NOTARY PUBLIC JOURNAL
LARGE ENTRIES

———————————————

Angelo Tropea

Copyright 2014 by Angelo Tropea. All rights reserved. No part of this book may be reproduced in any form or by electronic or mechanical means, including information storage and retrieval systems without permission in writing from the publisher.

ISBN 13: 978-1499378900
ISBN 10: 1499378904

Published by Angelo Tropea

This inexpensive journal provides for the recording of 250 large sized entries. It conveniently organizes the categories to be recorded and includes a "Notes" area for additional information.

Notaries Public…hold an office which can trace its origins back to ancient Rome when they were called *scribae, tabellius* or *notarius*. They are easily the oldest continuing branch of the legal profession worldwide.*

NOTARY PUBLIC JOURNAL – LARGE ENTRIES 3

1

Service: ☐ Acknowledgment ☐ Oath/Affirmation ☐ Jurat ☐ Other/See Notes   Fee $_____   Travel _____

Name (print)	Document type /Doc. name	Witness Name (print)	Date and Time Notarized _____ ___ _____ am / pm
Phone # / E-mail	Date of document	Witness Phone # / E-mail	Print of Right Thumb
Address	Satisfactory evidence of ID ☐ Driver's license ☐ Known Personally ☐ Credible Witness(es) ☐ Passport ☐ I.D. Card ☐ See Notes	Witness Address	
☐ ID. Issued by ☐ I.D. Number	☐ Expiration Date ☐ Issue Date	Notes	
Signer Signature		Witness Signature	

2

Service: ☐ Acknowledgment ☐ Oath/Affirmation ☐ Jurat ☐ Other/See Notes   Fee $_____   Travel _____

Name (print)	Document type /Doc. name	Witness Name (print)	Date and Time Notarized _____ ___ _____ am / pm
Phone # / E-mail	Date of document	Witness Phone # / E-mail	Print of Right Thumb
Address	Satisfactory evidence of ID ☐ Driver's license ☐ Known Personally ☐ Credible Witness(es) ☐ Passport ☐ I.D. Card ☐ See Notes	Witness Address	
☐ ID. Issued by ☐ I.D. Number	☐ Expiration Date ☐ Issue Date	Notes	
Signer Signature		Witness Signature	

4 | NOTARY PUBLIC JOURNAL – LARGE ENTRIES

3 | Service: ☐ Acknowledgment ☐ Oath/Affirmation ☐ Jurat ☐ Other/See Notes   Fee $_____   Travel_____

Name (print)	Document type /Doc. name	Witness Name (print)	Date and Time Notarized _____ ___ _____ am / pm
Phone # / E-mail	Date of document	Witness Phone # / E-mail	Print of Right Thumb
Address	Satisfactory evidence of ID ☐ Driver's license ☐ Known Personally ☐ Credible Witness(es) ☐ Passport ☐ I.D. Card ☐ See Notes	Witness Address	
☐ ID. Issued by ☐ I.D. Number	☐ Expiration Date ☐ Issue Date	Notes	
Signer Signature		Witness Signature	

4 | Service: ☐ Acknowledgment ☐ Oath/Affirmation ☐ Jurat ☐ Other/See Notes   Fee $_____   Travel_____

Name (print)	Document type /Doc. name	Witness Name (print)	Date and Time Notarized _____ ___ _____ am / pm
Phone # / E-mail	Date of document	Witness Phone # / E-mail	Print of Right Thumb
Address	Satisfactory evidence of ID ☐ Driver's license ☐ Known Personally ☐ Credible Witness(es) ☐ Passport ☐ I.D. Card ☐ See Notes	Witness Address	
☐ ID. Issued by ☐ I.D. Number	☐ Expiration Date ☐ Issue Date	Notes	
Signer Signature		Witness Signature	

NOTARY PUBLIC JOURNAL – LARGE ENTRIES | 5

5

Service: ☐ **Acknowledgment** ☐ **Oath/Affirmation** ☐ **Jurat** ☐ **Other/See Notes** Fee $_____ Travel_____

Name (print)	Document type /Doc. name	Witness Name (print)	Date and Time Notarized
			_____ ___ _____ am / pm
Phone # / E-mail	Date of document	Witness Phone # / E-mail	Print of Right Thumb
Address	Satisfactory evidence of ID ☐ Driver's license ☐ Known Personally ☐ Credible Witness(es) ☐ Passport ☐ I.D. Card ☐ See Notes	Witness Address	
☐ ID. Issued by ☐ I.D. Number	☐ Expiration Date ☐ Issue Date	Notes	
Signer Signature		Witness Signature	

6

Service: ☐ **Acknowledgment** ☐ **Oath/Affirmation** ☐ **Jurat** ☐ **Other/See Notes** Fee $_____ Travel_____

Name (print)	Document type /Doc. name	Witness Name (print)	Date and Time Notarized
			_____ ___ _____ am / pm
Phone # / E-mail	Date of document	Witness Phone # / E-mail	Print of Right Thumb
Address	Satisfactory evidence of ID ☐ Driver's license ☐ Known Personally ☐ Credible Witness(es) ☐ Passport ☐ I.D. Card ☐ See Notes	Witness Address	
☐ ID. Issued by ☐ I.D. Number	☐ Expiration Date ☐ Issue Date	Notes	
Signer Signature		Witness Signature	

6 | NOTARY PUBLIC JOURNAL – LARGE ENTRIES

7 | Service: ☐ Acknowledgment ☐ Oath/Affirmation ☐ Jurat ☐ Other/See Notes   Fee $_____   Travel_____

Name (print)	Document type /Doc. name	Witness Name (print)	Date and Time Notarized _____ ___ _____ am / pm
Phone # / E-mail	Date of document	Witness Phone # / E-mail	Print of Right Thumb
Address	Satisfactory evidence of ID ☐ Driver's license ☐ Known Personally ☐ Credible Witness(es) ☐ Passport ☐ I.D. Card ☐ See Notes	Witness Address	
☐ ID. Issued by .... ☐ I.D. Number	☐ Expiration Date .... ☐ Issue Date	Notes	
Signer Signature		Witness Signature	

8 | Service: ☐ Acknowledgment ☐ Oath/Affirmation ☐ Jurat ☐ Other/See Notes   Fee $_____   Travel_____

Name (print)	Document type /Doc. name	Witness Name (print)	Date and Time Notarized _____ ___ _____ am / pm
Phone # / E-mail	Date of document	Witness Phone # / E-mail	Print of Right Thumb
Address	Satisfactory evidence of ID ☐ Driver's license ☐ Known Personally ☐ Credible Witness(es) ☐ Passport ☐ I.D. Card ☐ See Notes	Witness Address	
☐ ID. Issued by .... ☐ I.D. Number	☐ Expiration Date .... ☐ Issue Date	Notes	
Signer Signature		Witness Signature	

NOTARY PUBLIC JOURNAL – LARGE ENTRIES 7

9

Service: ☐ Acknowledgment ☐ Oath/Affirmation ☐ Jurat ☐ Other/See Notes Fee $_____ Travel_____

Name (print)	Document type /Doc. name	Witness Name (print)	Date and Time Notarized _____ ___ _____ am / pm
Phone # / E-mail	Date of document	Witness Phone # / E-mail	Print of Right Thumb
Address	Satisfactory evidence of ID ☐ Driver's license ☐ Known Personally ☐ Credible Witness(es) ☐ Passport ☐ I.D. Card ☐ See Notes	Witness Address	
☐ ID. Issued by ☐ I.D. Number	☐ Expiration Date ☐ Issue Date	Notes	
Signer Signature		Witness Signature	

10

Service: ☐ Acknowledgment ☐ Oath/Affirmation ☐ Jurat ☐ Other/See Notes Fee $_____ Travel_____

Name (print)	Document type /Doc. name	Witness Name (print)	Date and Time Notarized _____ ___ _____ am / pm
Phone # / E-mail	Date of document	Witness Phone # / E-mail	Print of Right Thumb
Address	Satisfactory evidence of ID ☐ Driver's license ☐ Known Personally ☐ Credible Witness(es) ☐ Passport ☐ I.D. Card ☐ See Notes	Witness Address	
☐ ID. Issued by ☐ I.D. Number	☐ Expiration Date ☐ Issue Date	Notes	
Signer Signature		Witness Signature	

8 | NOTARY PUBLIC JOURNAL – LARGE ENTRIES

11 Service: ☐ Acknowledgment ☐ Oath/Affirmation ☐ Jurat ☐ Other/See Notes   Fee $_____   Travel_____

Name (print)	Document type /Doc. name	Witness Name (print)	Date and Time Notarized _____ ___ _____ am / pm
Phone # / E-mail	Date of document	Witness Phone # / E-mail	Print of Right Thumb
Address	Satisfactory evidence of ID ☐ Driver's license ☐ Known Personally ☐ Credible Witness(es) ☐ Passport ☐ I.D. Card ☐ See Notes	Witness Address	
☐ ID. Issued by ☐ I.D. Number	☐ Expiration Date ☐ Issue Date	Notes	
Signer Signature		Witness Signature	

12 Service: ☐ Acknowledgment ☐ Oath/Affirmation ☐ Jurat ☐ Other/See Notes   Fee $_____   Travel_____

Name (print)	Document type /Doc. name	Witness Name (print)	Date and Time Notarized _____ ___ _____ am / pm
Phone # / E-mail	Date of document	Witness Phone # / E-mail	Print of Right Thumb
Address	Satisfactory evidence of ID ☐ Driver's license ☐ Known Personally ☐ Credible Witness(es) ☐ Passport ☐ I.D. Card ☐ See Notes	Witness Address	
☐ ID. Issued by ☐ I.D. Number	☐ Expiration Date ☐ Issue Date	Notes	
Signer Signature		Witness Signature	

13

Service: ☐ Acknowledgment ☐ Oath/Affirmation ☐ Jurat ☐ Other/See Notes   Fee $_____   Travel_____

Name (print)	Document type /Doc. name	Witness Name (print)	Date and Time Notarized _____ ___ _____ am / pm
Phone # / E-mail	Date of document	Witness Phone # / E-mail	Print of Right Thumb
Address	Satisfactory evidence of ID ☐ Driver's license ☐ Known Personally ☐ Credible Witness(es) ☐ Passport ☐ I.D. Card ☐ See Notes	Witness Address	
☐ ID. Issued by ☐ I.D. Number	☐ Expiration Date ☐ Issue Date	Notes	
Signer Signature		Witness Signature	

14

Service: ☐ Acknowledgment ☐ Oath/Affirmation ☐ Jurat ☐ Other/See Notes   Fee $_____   Travel_____

Name (print)	Document type /Doc. name	Witness Name (print)	Date and Time Notarized _____ ___ _____ am / pm
Phone # / E-mail	Date of document	Witness Phone # / E-mail	Print of Right Thumb
Address	Satisfactory evidence of ID ☐ Driver's license ☐ Known Personally ☐ Credible Witness(es) ☐ Passport ☐ I.D. Card ☐ See Notes	Witness Address	
☐ ID. Issued by ☐ I.D. Number	☐ Expiration Date ☐ Issue Date	Notes	
Signer Signature		Witness Signature	

NOTARY PUBLIC JOURNAL – LARGE ENTRIES

15
Service: ☐ Acknowledgment ☐ Oath/Affirmation ☐ Jurat ☐ Other/See Notes   Fee $_____   Travel_____

Name (print)	Document type /Doc. name	Witness Name (print)	Date and Time Notarized _____ ___ _____ am / pm
Phone # / E-mail	Date of document	Witness Phone # / E-mail	Print of Right Thumb
Address	Satisfactory evidence of ID ☐ Driver's license ☐ Known Personally ☐ Credible Witness(es) ☐ Passport ☐ I.D. Card ☐ See Notes	Witness Address	
☐ ID. Issued by ☐ I.D. Number	☐ Expiration Date ☐ Issue Date	Notes	
Signer Signature		Witness Signature	

16
Service: ☐ Acknowledgment ☐ Oath/Affirmation ☐ Jurat ☐ Other/See Notes   Fee $_____   Travel_____

Name (print)	Document type /Doc. name	Witness Name (print)	Date and Time Notarized _____ ___ _____ am / pm
Phone # / E-mail	Date of document	Witness Phone # / E-mail	Print of Right Thumb
Address	Satisfactory evidence of ID ☐ Driver's license ☐ Known Personally ☐ Credible Witness(es) ☐ Passport ☐ I.D. Card ☐ See Notes	Witness Address	
☐ ID. Issued by ☐ I.D. Number	☐ Expiration Date ☐ Issue Date	Notes	
Signer Signature		Witness Signature	

NOTARY PUBLIC JOURNAL – LARGE ENTRIES | 11

17
Service: ☐ Acknowledgment ☐ Oath/Affirmation ☐ Jurat ☐ Other/See Notes   Fee $_____   Travel_____

Name (print)	Document type /Doc. name	Witness Name (print)	Date and Time Notarized _____ ___ _____ am / pm
Phone # / E-mail	Date of document	Witness Phone # / E-mail	Print of Right Thumb
Address	Satisfactory evidence of ID ☐ Driver's license ☐ Known Personally ☐ Credible Witness(es) ☐ Passport ☐ I.D. Card ☐ See Notes	Witness Address	
☐ ID. Issued by ☐ I.D. Number	☐ Expiration Date ☐ Issue Date	Notes	
Signer Signature		Witness Signature	

18
Service: ☐ Acknowledgment ☐ Oath/Affirmation ☐ Jurat ☐ Other/See Notes   Fee $_____   Travel_____

Name (print)	Document type /Doc. name	Witness Name (print)	Date and Time Notarized _____ ___ _____ am / pm
Phone # / E-mail	Date of document	Witness Phone # / E-mail	Print of Right Thumb
Address	Satisfactory evidence of ID ☐ Driver's license ☐ Known Personally ☐ Credible Witness(es) ☐ Passport ☐ I.D. Card ☐ See Notes	Witness Address	
☐ ID. Issued by ☐ I.D. Number	☐ Expiration Date ☐ Issue Date	Notes	
Signer Signature		Witness Signature	

NOTARY PUBLIC JOURNAL – LARGE ENTRIES

19
Service: ☐ Acknowledgment ☐ Oath/Affirmation ☐ Jurat ☐ Other/See Notes Fee $ _____ Travel _____

Name (print)	Document type /Doc. name	Witness Name (print)	Date and Time Notarized _____ ___ _____ am / pm
Phone # / E-mail	Date of document	Witness Phone # / E-mail	Print of Right Thumb
Address	Satisfactory evidence of ID ☐ Driver's license ☐ Known Personally ☐ Credible Witness(es) ☐ Passport ☐ I.D. Card ☐ See Notes	Witness Address	
☐ ID. Issued by ☐ I.D. Number	☐ Expiration Date ☐ Issue Date	Notes	
Signer Signature		Witness Signature	

20
Service: ☐ Acknowledgment ☐ Oath/Affirmation ☐ Jurat ☐ Other/See Notes Fee $ _____ Travel _____

Name (print)	Document type /Doc. name	Witness Name (print)	Date and Time Notarized _____ ___ _____ am / pm
Phone # / E-mail	Date of document	Witness Phone # / E-mail	Print of Right Thumb
Address	Satisfactory evidence of ID ☐ Driver's license ☐ Known Personally ☐ Credible Witness(es) ☐ Passport ☐ I.D. Card ☐ See Notes	Witness Address	
☐ ID. Issued by ☐ I.D. Number	☐ Expiration Date ☐ Issue Date	Notes	
Signer Signature		Witness Signature	

NOTARY PUBLIC JOURNAL – LARGE ENTRIES | 13

21 | Service: ☐ Acknowledgment ☐ Oath/Affirmation ☐ Jurat ☐ Other/See Notes   Fee $_____   Travel_____

Name (print)	Document type /Doc. name	Witness Name (print)	Date and Time Notarized _____ ___ _____ am / pm
Phone # / E-mail	Date of document	Witness Phone # / E-mail	Print of Right Thumb
Address	Satisfactory evidence of ID ☐ Driver's license ☐ Known Personally ☐ Credible Witness(es) ☐ Passport ☐ I.D. Card ☐ See Notes	Witness Address	
☐ ID. Issued by ☐ I.D. Number	☐ Expiration Date ☐ Issue Date	Notes	
Signer Signature		Witness Signature	

22 | Service: ☐ Acknowledgment ☐ Oath/Affirmation ☐ Jurat ☐ Other/See Notes   Fee $_____   Travel_____

Name (print)	Document type /Doc. name	Witness Name (print)	Date and Time Notarized _____ ___ _____ am / pm
Phone # / E-mail	Date of document	Witness Phone # / E-mail	Print of Right Thumb
Address	Satisfactory evidence of ID ☐ Driver's license ☐ Known Personally ☐ Credible Witness(es) ☐ Passport ☐ I.D. Card ☐ See Notes	Witness Address	
☐ ID. Issued by ☐ I.D. Number	☐ Expiration Date ☐ Issue Date	Notes	
Signer Signature		Witness Signature	

14 NOTARY PUBLIC JOURNAL – LARGE ENTRIES

23
Service: ☐ Acknowledgment ☐ Oath/Affirmation ☐ Jurat ☐ Other/See Notes   Fee $_____   Travel_____

Name (print)	Document type /Doc. name	Witness Name (print)	Date and Time Notarized _____ ___ _____ am / pm
Phone # / E-mail	Date of document	Witness Phone # / E-mail	Print of Right Thumb
Address	Satisfactory evidence of ID ☐ Driver's license ☐ Known Personally ☐ Credible Witness(es) ☐ Passport ☐ I.D. Card ☐ See Notes	Witness Address	
☐ ID. Issued by ☐ I.D. Number	☐ Expiration Date ☐ Issue Date	Notes	
Signer Signature		Witness Signature	

24
Service: ☐ Acknowledgment ☐ Oath/Affirmation ☐ Jurat ☐ Other/See Notes   Fee $_____   Travel_____

Name (print)	Document type /Doc. name	Witness Name (print)	Date and Time Notarized _____ ___ _____ am / pm
Phone # / E-mail	Date of document	Witness Phone # / E-mail	Print of Right Thumb
Address	Satisfactory evidence of ID ☐ Driver's license ☐ Known Personally ☐ Credible Witness(es) ☐ Passport ☐ I.D. Card ☐ See Notes	Witness Address	
☐ ID. Issued by ☐ I.D. Number	☐ Expiration Date ☐ Issue Date	Notes	
Signer Signature		Witness Signature	

NOTARY PUBLIC JOURNAL – LARGE ENTRIES | 15

25
Service: ☐ Acknowledgment ☐ Oath/Affirmation ☐ Jurat ☐ Other/See Notes Fee $_____ Travel_____

Name (print)	Document type /Doc. name	Witness Name (print)	Date and Time Notarized _____ ___ _____ am / pm
Phone # / E-mail	Date of document	Witness Phone # / E-mail	Print of Right Thumb
Address	Satisfactory evidence of ID ☐ Driver's license ☐ Known Personally ☐ Credible Witness(es) ☐ Passport ☐ I.D. Card ☐ See Notes	Witness Address	
☐ ID. Issued by ☐ I.D. Number	☐ Expiration Date ☐ Issue Date	Notes	
Signer Signature		Witness Signature	

26
Service: ☐ Acknowledgment ☐ Oath/Affirmation ☐ Jurat ☐ Other/See Notes Fee $_____ Travel_____

Name (print)	Document type /Doc. name	Witness Name (print)	Date and Time Notarized _____ ___ _____ am / pm
Phone # / E-mail	Date of document	Witness Phone # / E-mail	Print of Right Thumb
Address	Satisfactory evidence of ID ☐ Driver's license ☐ Known Personally ☐ Credible Witness(es) ☐ Passport ☐ I.D. Card ☐ See Notes	Witness Address	
☐ ID. Issued by ☐ I.D. Number	☐ Expiration Date ☐ Issue Date	Notes	
Signer Signature		Witness Signature	

16 | NOTARY PUBLIC JOURNAL – LARGE ENTRIES

27 | Service: ☐ Acknowledgment ☐ Oath/Affirmation ☐ Jurat ☐ Other/See Notes   Fee $_____   Travel_____

Name (print)	Document type /Doc. name	Witness Name (print)	Date and Time Notarized
			_____ ___ _____ am / pm
Phone # / E-mail	Date of document	Witness Phone # / E-mail	Print of Right Thumb
Address	Satisfactory evidence of ID ☐ Driver's license ☐ Known Personally ☐ Credible Witness(es) ☐ Passport ☐ I.D. Card ☐ See Notes	Witness Address	
☐ ID. Issued by ☐ I.D. Number	☐ Expiration Date ☐ Issue Date	Notes	
Signer Signature		Witness Signature	

28 | Service: ☐ Acknowledgment ☐ Oath/Affirmation ☐ Jurat ☐ Other/See Notes   Fee $_____   Travel_____

Name (print)	Document type /Doc. name	Witness Name (print)	Date and Time Notarized
			_____ ___ _____ am / pm
Phone # / E-mail	Date of document	Witness Phone # / E-mail	Print of Right Thumb
Address	Satisfactory evidence of ID ☐ Driver's license ☐ Known Personally ☐ Credible Witness(es) ☐ Passport ☐ I.D. Card ☐ See Notes	Witness Address	
☐ ID. Issued by ☐ I.D. Number	☐ Expiration Date ☐ Issue Date	Notes	
Signer Signature		Witness Signature	

NOTARY PUBLIC JOURNAL – LARGE ENTRIES   17

29

Service: ☐ **Acknowledgment**   ☐ **Oath/Affirmation**   ☐ **Jurat**   ☐ **Other/See Notes**   Fee $_____   Travel_____

Name (print)	Document type /Doc. name	Witness Name (print)	Date and Time Notarized _____ ___ _____ am / pm
Phone # / E-mail	Date of document	Witness Phone # / E-mail	Print of Right Thumb
Address	Satisfactory evidence of ID ☐ Driver's license ☐ Known Personally ☐ Credible Witness(es) ☐ Passport ☐ I.D. Card ☐ See Notes	Witness Address	
☐ ID. Issued by ☐ I.D. Number	☐ Expiration Date ☐ Issue Date	Notes	
Signer Signature		Witness Signature	

30

Service: ☐ **Acknowledgment**   ☐ **Oath/Affirmation**   ☐ **Jurat**   ☐ **Other/See Notes**   Fee $_____   Travel_____

Name (print)	Document type /Doc. name	Witness Name (print)	Date and Time Notarized _____ ___ _____ am / pm
Phone # / E-mail	Date of document	Witness Phone # / E-mail	Print of Right Thumb
Address	Satisfactory evidence of ID ☐ Driver's license ☐ Known Personally ☐ Credible Witness(es) ☐ Passport ☐ I.D. Card ☐ See Notes	Witness Address	
☐ ID. Issued by ☐ I.D. Number	☐ Expiration Date ☐ Issue Date	Notes	
Signer Signature		Witness Signature	

NOTARY PUBLIC JOURNAL – LARGE ENTRIES

31

Service: ☐ Acknowledgment ☐ Oath/Affirmation ☐ Jurat ☐ Other/See Notes   Fee $_____   Travel_____

Name (print)	Document type /Doc. name	Witness Name (print)	Date and Time Notarized _____ ____ _____ am / pm
Phone # / E-mail	Date of document	Witness Phone # / E-mail	Print of Right Thumb
Address	Satisfactory evidence of ID ☐ Driver's license ☐ Known Personally ☐ Credible Witness(es) ☐ Passport ☐ I.D. Card ☐ See Notes	Witness Address	
☐ ID. Issued by ☐ I.D. Number	☐ Expiration Date ☐ Issue Date	Notes	
Signer Signature		Witness Signature	

32

Service: ☐ Acknowledgment ☐ Oath/Affirmation ☐ Jurat ☐ Other/See Notes   Fee $_____   Travel_____

Name (print)	Document type /Doc. name	Witness Name (print)	Date and Time Notarized _____ ____ _____ am / pm
Phone # / E-mail	Date of document	Witness Phone # / E-mail	Print of Right Thumb
Address	Satisfactory evidence of ID ☐ Driver's license ☐ Known Personally ☐ Credible Witness(es) ☐ Passport ☐ I.D. Card ☐ See Notes	Witness Address	
☐ ID. Issued by ☐ I.D. Number	☐ Expiration Date ☐ Issue Date	Notes	
Signer Signature		Witness Signature	

NOTARY PUBLIC JOURNAL – LARGE ENTRIES   19

33 Service: ☐ Acknowledgment ☐ Oath/Affirmation ☐ Jurat ☐ Other/See Notes   Fee $_____   Travel_____

Name (print)	Document type /Doc. name	Witness Name (print)	Date and Time Notarized _____ ___ _____ am / pm
Phone # / E-mail	Date of document	Witness Phone # / E-mail	Print of Right Thumb
Address	Satisfactory evidence of ID ☐ Driver's license ☐ Known Personally ☐ Credible Witness(es) ☐ Passport ☐ I.D. Card ☐ See Notes	Witness Address	
☐ ID. Issued by ☐ I.D. Number	☐ Expiration Date ☐ Issue Date	Notes	
Signer Signature		Witness Signature	

34 Service: ☐ Acknowledgment ☐ Oath/Affirmation ☐ Jurat ☐ Other/See Notes   Fee $_____   Travel_____

Name (print)	Document type /Doc. name	Witness Name (print)	Date and Time Notarized _____ ___ _____ am / pm
Phone # / E-mail	Date of document	Witness Phone # / E-mail	Print of Right Thumb
Address	Satisfactory evidence of ID ☐ Driver's license ☐ Known Personally ☐ Credible Witness(es) ☐ Passport ☐ I.D. Card ☐ See Notes	Witness Address	
☐ ID. Issued by ☐ I.D. Number	☐ Expiration Date ☐ Issue Date	Notes	
Signer Signature		Witness Signature	

NOTARY PUBLIC JOURNAL – LARGE ENTRIES

35

Service: ☐ Acknowledgment ☐ Oath/Affirmation ☐ Jurat ☐ Other/See Notes   Fee $_____   Travel_____

Name (print)	Document type /Doc. name	Witness Name (print)	Date and Time Notarized _____ ___ _____ am / pm
Phone # / E-mail	Date of document	Witness Phone # / E-mail	Print of Right Thumb
Address	Satisfactory evidence of ID ☐ Driver's license ☐ Known Personally ☐ Credible Witness(es) ☐ Passport ☐ I.D. Card ☐ See Notes	Witness Address	
☐ ID. Issued by ☐ I.D. Number	☐ Expiration Date ☐ Issue Date	Notes	
Signer Signature		Witness Signature	

36

Service: ☐ Acknowledgment ☐ Oath/Affirmation ☐ Jurat ☐ Other/See Notes   Fee $_____   Travel_____

Name (print)	Document type /Doc. name	Witness Name (print)	Date and Time Notarized _____ ___ _____ am / pm
Phone # / E-mail	Date of document	Witness Phone # / E-mail	Print of Right Thumb
Address	Satisfactory evidence of ID ☐ Driver's license ☐ Known Personally ☐ Credible Witness(es) ☐ Passport ☐ I.D. Card ☐ See Notes	Witness Address	
☐ ID. Issued by ☐ I.D. Number	☐ Expiration Date ☐ Issue Date	Notes	
Signer Signature		Witness Signature	

NOTARY PUBLIC JOURNAL – LARGE ENTRIES | 21

37

Service: ☐ Acknowledgment ☐ Oath/Affirmation ☐ Jurat ☐ Other/See Notes Fee $_____ Travel_____

Name (print)	Document type /Doc. name	Witness Name (print)	Date and Time Notarized _____ ____ _____ am / pm
Phone # / E-mail	Date of document	Witness Phone # / E-mail	Print of Right Thumb
Address	Satisfactory evidence of ID ☐ Driver's license ☐ Known Personally ☐ Credible Witness(es) ☐ Passport ☐ I.D. Card ☐ See Notes	Witness Address	
☐ ID. Issued by ☐ I.D. Number	☐ Expiration Date ☐ Issue Date	Notes	
Signer Signature		Witness Signature	

38

Service: ☐ Acknowledgment ☐ Oath/Affirmation ☐ Jurat ☐ Other/See Notes Fee $_____ Travel_____

Name (print)	Document type /Doc. name	Witness Name (print)	Date and Time Notarized _____ ____ _____ am / pm
Phone # / E-mail	Date of document	Witness Phone # / E-mail	Print of Right Thumb
Address	Satisfactory evidence of ID ☐ Driver's license ☐ Known Personally ☐ Credible Witness(es) ☐ Passport ☐ I.D. Card ☐ See Notes	Witness Address	
☐ ID. Issued by ☐ I.D. Number	☐ Expiration Date ☐ Issue Date	Notes	
Signer Signature		Witness Signature	

NOTARY PUBLIC JOURNAL – LARGE ENTRIES

39

Service: ☐ Acknowledgment ☐ Oath/Affirmation ☐ Jurat ☐ Other/See Notes Fee $_____ Travel_____

Name (print)	Document type /Doc. name	Witness Name (print)	Date and Time Notarized _____ ___ _____ am / pm
Phone # / E-mail	Date of document	Witness Phone # / E-mail	Print of Right Thumb
Address	Satisfactory evidence of ID ☐ Driver's license ☐ Known Personally ☐ Credible Witness(es) ☐ Passport ☐ I.D. Card ☐ See Notes	Witness Address	
☐ ID. Issued by ☐ I.D. Number	☐ Expiration Date ☐ Issue Date	Notes	
Signer Signature		Witness Signature	

40

Service: ☐ Acknowledgment ☐ Oath/Affirmation ☐ Jurat ☐ Other/See Notes Fee $_____ Travel_____

Name (print)	Document type /Doc. name	Witness Name (print)	Date and Time Notarized _____ ___ _____ am / pm
Phone # / E-mail	Date of document	Witness Phone # / E-mail	Print of Right Thumb
Address	Satisfactory evidence of ID ☐ Driver's license ☐ Known Personally ☐ Credible Witness(es) ☐ Passport ☐ I.D. Card ☐ See Notes	Witness Address	
☐ ID. Issued by ☐ I.D. Number	☐ Expiration Date ☐ Issue Date	Notes	
Signer Signature		Witness Signature	

NOTARY PUBLIC JOURNAL – LARGE ENTRIES   23

41
Service: ☐ Acknowledgment ☐ Oath/Affirmation ☐ Jurat ☐ Other/See Notes   Fee $_____ Travel_____

Name (print)	Document type /Doc. name	Witness Name (print)	Date and Time Notarized _____ ___ _____ am / pm
Phone # / E-mail	Date of document	Witness Phone # / E-mail	Print of Right Thumb
Address	Satisfactory evidence of ID ☐ Driver's license ☐ Known Personally ☐ Credible Witness(es) ☐ Passport ☐ I.D. Card ☐ See Notes	Witness Address	
☐ ID. Issued by ☐ I.D. Number	☐ Expiration Date ☐ Issue Date	Notes	
Signer Signature		Witness Signature	

42
Service: ☐ Acknowledgment ☐ Oath/Affirmation ☐ Jurat ☐ Other/See Notes   Fee $_____ Travel_____

Name (print)	Document type /Doc. name	Witness Name (print)	Date and Time Notarized _____ ___ _____ am / pm
Phone # / E-mail	Date of document	Witness Phone # / E-mail	Print of Right Thumb
Address	Satisfactory evidence of ID ☐ Driver's license ☐ Known Personally ☐ Credible Witness(es) ☐ Passport ☐ I.D. Card ☐ See Notes	Witness Address	
☐ ID. Issued by ☐ I.D. Number	☐ Expiration Date ☐ Issue Date	Notes	
Signer Signature		Witness Signature	

NOTARY PUBLIC JOURNAL – LARGE ENTRIES

43

Service: ☐ **Acknowledgment** ☐ **Oath/Affirmation** ☐ **Jurat** ☐ **Other/See Notes** Fee $_____ Travel_____

Name (print)	Document type /Doc. name	Witness Name (print)	Date and Time Notarized _____ ___ _____ am / pm
Phone # / E-mail	Date of document	Witness Phone # / E-mail	Print of Right Thumb
Address	Satisfactory evidence of ID ☐ Driver's license ☐ Known Personally ☐ Credible Witness(es) ☐ Passport ☐ I.D. Card ☐ See Notes	Witness Address	
☐ ID. Issued by ☐ I.D. Number	☐ Expiration Date ☐ Issue Date	Notes	
Signer Signature		Witness Signature	

44

Service: ☐ **Acknowledgment** ☐ **Oath/Affirmation** ☐ **Jurat** ☐ **Other/See Notes** Fee $_____ Travel_____

Name (print)	Document type /Doc. name	Witness Name (print)	Date and Time Notarized _____ ___ _____ am / pm
Phone # / E-mail	Date of document	Witness Phone # / E-mail	Print of Right Thumb
Address	Satisfactory evidence of ID ☐ Driver's license ☐ Known Personally ☐ Credible Witness(es) ☐ Passport ☐ I.D. Card ☐ See Notes	Witness Address	
☐ ID. Issued by ☐ I.D. Number	☐ Expiration Date ☐ Issue Date	Notes	
Signer Signature		Witness Signature	

NOTARY PUBLIC JOURNAL – LARGE ENTRIES | 25

45
Service: ☐ Acknowledgment ☐ Oath/Affirmation ☐ Jurat ☐ Other/See Notes Fee $_____ Travel_____

Name (print)	Document type /Doc. name	Witness Name (print)	Date and Time Notarized _____ ___ _____ am / pm
Phone # / E-mail	Date of document	Witness Phone # / E-mail	Print of Right Thumb
Address	Satisfactory evidence of ID ☐ Driver's license ☐ Known Personally ☐ Credible Witness(es) ☐ Passport ☐ I.D. Card ☐ See Notes	Witness Address	
☐ ID. Issued by ☐ I.D. Number	☐ Expiration Date ☐ Issue Date	Notes	
Signer Signature		Witness Signature	

46
Service: ☐ Acknowledgment ☐ Oath/Affirmation ☐ Jurat ☐ Other/See Notes Fee $_____ Travel_____

Name (print)	Document type /Doc. name	Witness Name (print)	Date and Time Notarized _____ ___ _____ am / pm
Phone # / E-mail	Date of document	Witness Phone # / E-mail	Print of Right Thumb
Address	Satisfactory evidence of ID ☐ Driver's license ☐ Known Personally ☐ Credible Witness(es) ☐ Passport ☐ I.D. Card ☐ See Notes	Witness Address	
☐ ID. Issued by ☐ I.D. Number	☐ Expiration Date ☐ Issue Date	Notes	
Signer Signature		Witness Signature	

NOTARY PUBLIC JOURNAL – LARGE ENTRIES

47

Service: ☐ Acknowledgment ☐ Oath/Affirmation ☐ Jurat ☐ Other/See Notes   Fee $ _____ Travel _____

Name (print)	Document type /Doc. name	Witness Name (print)	Date and Time Notarized _____ ___ _____ am / pm
Phone # / E-mail	Date of document	Witness Phone # / E-mail	Print of Right Thumb
Address	Satisfactory evidence of ID ☐ Driver's license ☐ Known Personally ☐ Credible Witness(es) ☐ Passport ☐ I.D. Card ☐ See Notes	Witness Address	
☐ ID. Issued by ☐ I.D. Number	☐ Expiration Date ☐ Issue Date	Notes	
Signer Signature		Witness Signature	

48

Service: ☐ Acknowledgment ☐ Oath/Affirmation ☐ Jurat ☐ Other/See Notes   Fee $ _____ Travel _____

Name (print)	Document type /Doc. name	Witness Name (print)	Date and Time Notarized _____ ___ _____ am / pm
Phone # / E-mail	Date of document	Witness Phone # / E-mail	Print of Right Thumb
Address	Satisfactory evidence of ID ☐ Driver's license ☐ Known Personally ☐ Credible Witness(es) ☐ Passport ☐ I.D. Card ☐ See Notes	Witness Address	
☐ ID. Issued by ☐ I.D. Number	☐ Expiration Date ☐ Issue Date	Notes	
Signer Signature		Witness Signature	

NOTARY PUBLIC JOURNAL – LARGE ENTRIES

49

Service: ☐ Acknowledgment ☐ Oath/Affirmation ☐ Jurat ☐ Other/See Notes Fee $_____ Travel_____

Name (print)	Document type /Doc. name	Witness Name (print)	Date and Time Notarized _____ ___ _____ am / pm
Phone # / E-mail	Date of document	Witness Phone # / E-mail	Print of Right Thumb
Address	Satisfactory evidence of ID ☐ Driver's license ☐ Known Personally ☐ Credible Witness(es) ☐ Passport ☐ I.D. Card ☐ See Notes	Witness Address	
☐ ID. Issued by ☐ I.D. Number	☐ Expiration Date ☐ Issue Date	Notes	
Signer Signature		Witness Signature	

50

Service: ☐ Acknowledgment ☐ Oath/Affirmation ☐ Jurat ☐ Other/See Notes Fee $_____ Travel_____

Name (print)	Document type /Doc. name	Witness Name (print)	Date and Time Notarized _____ ___ _____ am / pm
Phone # / E-mail	Date of document	Witness Phone # / E-mail	Print of Right Thumb
Address	Satisfactory evidence of ID ☐ Driver's license ☐ Known Personally ☐ Credible Witness(es) ☐ Passport ☐ I.D. Card ☐ See Notes	Witness Address	
☐ ID. Issued by ☐ I.D. Number	☐ Expiration Date ☐ Issue Date	Notes	
Signer Signature		Witness Signature	

NOTARY PUBLIC JOURNAL – LARGE ENTRIES

51

Service: ☐ Acknowledgment ☐ Oath/Affirmation ☐ Jurat ☐ Other/See Notes   Fee $_____   Travel_____

Name (print)	Document type /Doc. name	Witness Name (print)	Date and Time Notarized _____ ___ _____ am / pm
Phone # / E-mail	Date of document	Witness Phone # / E-mail	Print of Right Thumb
Address	Satisfactory evidence of ID ☐ Driver's license ☐ Known Personally ☐ Credible Witness(es) ☐ Passport ☐ I.D. Card ☐ See Notes	Witness Address	
☐ ID. Issued by ☐ I.D. Number	☐ Expiration Date ☐ Issue Date	Notes	
Signer Signature		Witness Signature	

52

Service: ☐ Acknowledgment ☐ Oath/Affirmation ☐ Jurat ☐ Other/See Notes   Fee $_____   Travel_____

Name (print)	Document type /Doc. name	Witness Name (print)	Date and Time Notarized _____ ___ _____ am / pm
Phone # / E-mail	Date of document	Witness Phone # / E-mail	Print of Right Thumb
Address	Satisfactory evidence of ID ☐ Driver's license ☐ Known Personally ☐ Credible Witness(es) ☐ Passport ☐ I.D. Card ☐ See Notes	Witness Address	
☐ ID. Issued by ☐ I.D. Number	☐ Expiration Date ☐ Issue Date	Notes	
Signer Signature		Witness Signature	

NOTARY PUBLIC JOURNAL – LARGE ENTRIES

53

Service: ☐ Acknowledgment ☐ Oath/Affirmation ☐ Jurat ☐ Other/See Notes   Fee $_____   Travel_____

Name (print)	Document type /Doc. name	Witness Name (print)	Date and Time Notarized _____ ___ _____ am / pm
Phone # / E-mail	Date of document	Witness Phone # / E-mail	Print of Right Thumb
Address	Satisfactory evidence of ID ☐ Driver's license ☐ Known Personally ☐ Credible Witness(es) ☐ Passport ☐ I.D. Card ☐ See Notes	Witness Address	
☐ ID. Issued by ☐ I.D. Number	☐ Expiration Date ☐ Issue Date	Notes	
Signer Signature		Witness Signature	

54

Service: ☐ Acknowledgment ☐ Oath/Affirmation ☐ Jurat ☐ Other/See Notes   Fee $_____   Travel_____

Name (print)	Document type /Doc. name	Witness Name (print)	Date and Time Notarized _____ ___ _____ am / pm
Phone # / E-mail	Date of document	Witness Phone # / E-mail	Print of Right Thumb
Address	Satisfactory evidence of ID ☐ Driver's license ☐ Known Personally ☐ Credible Witness(es) ☐ Passport ☐ I.D. Card ☐ See Notes	Witness Address	
☐ ID. Issued by ☐ I.D. Number	☐ Expiration Date ☐ Issue Date	Notes	
Signer Signature		Witness Signature	

NOTARY PUBLIC JOURNAL – LARGE ENTRIES

55 | Service: ☐ Acknowledgment ☐ Oath/Affirmation ☐ Jurat ☐ Other/See Notes   Fee $_____   Travel_____

Name (print)	Document type /Doc. name	Witness Name (print)	Date and Time Notarized _____ ___ _____ am / pm
Phone # / E-mail	Date of document	Witness Phone # / E-mail	Print of Right Thumb
Address	Satisfactory evidence of ID ☐ Driver's license ☐ Known Personally ☐ Credible Witness(es) ☐ Passport ☐ I.D. Card ☐ See Notes	Witness Address	
☐ ID. Issued by ☐ I.D. Number	☐ Expiration Date ☐ Issue Date	Notes	
Signer Signature		Witness Signature	

56 | Service: ☐ Acknowledgment ☐ Oath/Affirmation ☐ Jurat ☐ Other/See Notes   Fee $_____   Travel_____

Name (print)	Document type /Doc. name	Witness Name (print)	Date and Time Notarized _____ ___ _____ am / pm
Phone # / E-mail	Date of document	Witness Phone # / E-mail	Print of Right Thumb
Address	Satisfactory evidence of ID ☐ Driver's license ☐ Known Personally ☐ Credible Witness(es) ☐ Passport ☐ I.D. Card ☐ See Notes	Witness Address	
☐ ID. Issued by ☐ I.D. Number	☐ Expiration Date ☐ Issue Date	Notes	
Signer Signature		Witness Signature	

NOTARY PUBLIC JOURNAL – LARGE ENTRIES

57
Service: ☐ Acknowledgment ☐ Oath/Affirmation ☐ Jurat ☐ Other/See Notes   Fee $_____   Travel_____

Name (print)	Document type /Doc. name	Witness Name (print)	Date and Time Notarized _____ ___ _____ am / pm
Phone # / E-mail	Date of document	Witness Phone # / E-mail	Print of Right Thumb
Address	Satisfactory evidence of ID ☐ Driver's license ☐ Known Personally ☐ Credible Witness(es) ☐ Passport ☐ I.D. Card ☐ See Notes	Witness Address	
☐ ID. Issued by ☐ I.D. Number	☐ Expiration Date ☐ Issue Date	Notes	
Signer Signature		Witness Signature	

58
Service: ☐ Acknowledgment ☐ Oath/Affirmation ☐ Jurat ☐ Other/See Notes   Fee $_____   Travel_____

Name (print)	Document type /Doc. name	Witness Name (print)	Date and Time Notarized _____ ___ _____ am / pm
Phone # / E-mail	Date of document	Witness Phone # / E-mail	Print of Right Thumb
Address	Satisfactory evidence of ID ☐ Driver's license ☐ Known Personally ☐ Credible Witness(es) ☐ Passport ☐ I.D. Card ☐ See Notes	Witness Address	
☐ ID. Issued by ☐ I.D. Number	☐ Expiration Date ☐ Issue Date	Notes	
Signer Signature		Witness Signature	

NOTARY PUBLIC JOURNAL – LARGE ENTRIES

59

Service: ☐ Acknowledgment ☐ Oath/Affirmation ☐ Jurat ☐ Other/See Notes   Fee $_____   Travel_____

Name (print)	Document type /Doc. name	Witness Name (print)	Date and Time Notarized _____ ___ _____ am / pm
Phone # / E-mail	Date of document	Witness Phone # / E-mail	Print of Right Thumb
Address	Satisfactory evidence of ID ☐ Driver's license ☐ Known Personally ☐ Credible Witness(es) ☐ Passport ☐ I.D. Card ☐ See Notes	Witness Address	
☐ ID. Issued by ☐ I.D. Number	☐ Expiration Date ☐ Issue Date	Notes	
Signer Signature		Witness Signature	

60

Service: ☐ Acknowledgment ☐ Oath/Affirmation ☐ Jurat ☐ Other/See Notes   Fee $_____   Travel_____

Name (print)	Document type /Doc. name	Witness Name (print)	Date and Time Notarized _____ ___ _____ am / pm
Phone # / E-mail	Date of document	Witness Phone # / E-mail	Print of Right Thumb
Address	Satisfactory evidence of ID ☐ Driver's license ☐ Known Personally ☐ Credible Witness(es) ☐ Passport ☐ I.D. Card ☐ See Notes	Witness Address	
☐ ID. Issued by ☐ I.D. Number	☐ Expiration Date ☐ Issue Date	Notes	
Signer Signature		Witness Signature	

NOTARY PUBLIC JOURNAL – LARGE ENTRIES | 33

61
Service: ☐ Acknowledgment ☐ Oath/Affirmation ☐ Jurat ☐ Other/See Notes Fee $_____ Travel _____

Name (print)	Document type /Doc. name	Witness Name (print)	Date and Time Notarized _____ ___ _____ am / pm
Phone # / E-mail	Date of document	Witness Phone # / E-mail	Print of Right Thumb
Address	Satisfactory evidence of ID ☐ Driver's license ☐ Known Personally ☐ Credible Witness(es) ☐ Passport ☐ I.D. Card ☐ See Notes	Witness Address	
☐ ID. Issued by ☐ I.D. Number	☐ Expiration Date ☐ Issue Date	Notes	
Signer Signature		Witness Signature	

62
Service: ☐ Acknowledgment ☐ Oath/Affirmation ☐ Jurat ☐ Other/See Notes Fee $_____ Travel _____

Name (print)	Document type /Doc. name	Witness Name (print)	Date and Time Notarized _____ ___ _____ am / pm
Phone # / E-mail	Date of document	Witness Phone # / E-mail	Print of Right Thumb
Address	Satisfactory evidence of ID ☐ Driver's license ☐ Known Personally ☐ Credible Witness(es) ☐ Passport ☐ I.D. Card ☐ See Notes	Witness Address	
☐ ID. Issued by ☐ I.D. Number	☐ Expiration Date ☐ Issue Date	Notes	
Signer Signature		Witness Signature	

NOTARY PUBLIC JOURNAL – LARGE ENTRIES

63

Service: ☐ Acknowledgment ☐ Oath/Affirmation ☐ Jurat ☐ Other/See Notes Fee $_____ Travel_____

Name (print)	Document type /Doc. name	Witness Name (print)	Date and Time Notarized
			_____ ___ _____ am / pm
Phone # / E-mail	Date of document	Witness Phone # / E-mail	Print of Right Thumb
Address	Satisfactory evidence of ID ☐ Driver's license ☐ Known Personally ☐ Credible Witness(es) ☐ Passport ☐ I.D. Card ☐ See Notes	Witness Address	
☐ ID. Issued by ☐ I.D. Number	☐ Expiration Date ☐ Issue Date	Notes	
Signer Signature		Witness Signature	

64

Service: ☐ Acknowledgment ☐ Oath/Affirmation ☐ Jurat ☐ Other/See Notes Fee $_____ Travel_____

Name (print)	Document type /Doc. name	Witness Name (print)	Date and Time Notarized
			_____ ___ _____ am / pm
Phone # / E-mail	Date of document	Witness Phone # / E-mail	Print of Right Thumb
Address	Satisfactory evidence of ID ☐ Driver's license ☐ Known Personally ☐ Credible Witness(es) ☐ Passport ☐ I.D. Card ☐ See Notes	Witness Address	
☐ ID. Issued by ☐ I.D. Number	☐ Expiration Date ☐ Issue Date	Notes	
Signer Signature		Witness Signature	

NOTARY PUBLIC JOURNAL – LARGE ENTRIES | 35

65
Service: ☐ Acknowledgment ☐ Oath/Affirmation ☐ Jurat ☐ Other/See Notes Fee $_____ Travel_____

Name (print)	Document type /Doc. name	Witness Name (print)	Date and Time Notarized _____ ___ _____ am / pm
Phone # / E-mail	Date of document	Witness Phone # / E-mail	Print of Right Thumb
Address	Satisfactory evidence of ID ☐ Driver's license ☐ Known Personally ☐ Credible Witness(es) ☐ Passport ☐ I.D. Card ☐ See Notes	Witness Address	
☐ ID. Issued by ☐ I.D. Number	☐ Expiration Date ☐ Issue Date	Notes	
Signer Signature		Witness Signature	

66
Service: ☐ Acknowledgment ☐ Oath/Affirmation ☐ Jurat ☐ Other/See Notes Fee $_____ Travel_____

Name (print)	Document type /Doc. name	Witness Name (print)	Date and Time Notarized _____ ___ _____ am / pm
Phone # / E-mail	Date of document	Witness Phone # / E-mail	Print of Right Thumb
Address	Satisfactory evidence of ID ☐ Driver's license ☐ Known Personally ☐ Credible Witness(es) ☐ Passport ☐ I.D. Card ☐ See Notes	Witness Address	
☐ ID. Issued by ☐ I.D. Number	☐ Expiration Date ☐ Issue Date	Notes	
Signer Signature		Witness Signature	

36 | NOTARY PUBLIC JOURNAL – LARGE ENTRIES

67

Service: ☐ Acknowledgment ☐ Oath/Affirmation ☐ Jurat ☐ Other/See Notes **Fee $**_____ **Travel**_____

Name (print)	Document type /Doc. name	Witness Name (print)	Date and Time Notarized _____ ___ _____ am / pm
Phone # / E-mail	Date of document	Witness Phone # / E-mail	Print of Right Thumb
Address	Satisfactory evidence of ID ☐ Driver's license ☐ Known Personally ☐ Credible Witness(es) ☐ Passport ☐ I.D. Card ☐ See Notes	Witness Address	
☐ ID. Issued by ☐ I.D. Number	☐ Expiration Date ☐ Issue Date	Notes	
Signer Signature		Witness Signature	

68

Service: ☐ Acknowledgment ☐ Oath/Affirmation ☐ Jurat ☐ Other/See Notes **Fee $**_____ **Travel**_____

Name (print)	Document type /Doc. name	Witness Name (print)	Date and Time Notarized _____ ___ _____ am / pm
Phone # / E-mail	Date of document	Witness Phone # / E-mail	Print of Right Thumb
Address	Satisfactory evidence of ID ☐ Driver's license ☐ Known Personally ☐ Credible Witness(es) ☐ Passport ☐ I.D. Card ☐ See Notes	Witness Address	
☐ ID. Issued by ☐ I.D. Number	☐ Expiration Date ☐ Issue Date	Notes	
Signer Signature		Witness Signature	

NOTARY PUBLIC JOURNAL – LARGE ENTRIES 37

69
Service: ☐ Acknowledgment ☐ Oath/Affirmation ☐ Jurat ☐ Other/See Notes **Fee $**_____ **Travel**_____

Name (print)	Document type /Doc. name	Witness Name (print)	Date and Time Notarized _____ ___ _____ am / pm
Phone # / E-mail	Date of document	Witness Phone # / E-mail	Print of Right Thumb
Address	Satisfactory evidence of ID ☐ Driver's license ☐ Known Personally ☐ Credible Witness(es) ☐ Passport ☐ I.D. Card ☐ See Notes	Witness Address	
☐ ID. Issued by ☐ I.D. Number	☐ Expiration Date ☐ Issue Date	Notes	
Signer Signature		Witness Signature	

70
Service: ☐ Acknowledgment ☐ Oath/Affirmation ☐ Jurat ☐ Other/See Notes **Fee $**_____ **Travel**_____

Name (print)	Document type /Doc. name	Witness Name (print)	Date and Time Notarized _____ ___ _____ am / pm
Phone # / E-mail	Date of document	Witness Phone # / E-mail	Print of Right Thumb
Address	Satisfactory evidence of ID ☐ Driver's license ☐ Known Personally ☐ Credible Witness(es) ☐ Passport ☐ I.D. Card ☐ See Notes	Witness Address	
☐ ID. Issued by ☐ I.D. Number	☐ Expiration Date ☐ Issue Date	Notes	
Signer Signature		Witness Signature	

NOTARY PUBLIC JOURNAL – LARGE ENTRIES

71

Service: ☐ Acknowledgment ☐ Oath/Affirmation ☐ Jurat ☐ Other/See Notes Fee $_____ Travel_____

Name (print)	Document type /Doc. name	Witness Name (print)	Date and Time Notarized
			_____ ___ _____ am / pm
Phone # / E-mail	Date of document	Witness Phone # / E-mail	Print of Right Thumb
Address	Satisfactory evidence of ID ☐ Driver's license ☐ Known Personally ☐ Credible Witness(es) ☐ Passport ☐ I.D. Card ☐ See Notes	Witness Address	
☐ ID. Issued by ☐ I.D. Number	☐ Expiration Date ☐ Issue Date	Notes	
Signer Signature		Witness Signature	

72

Service: ☐ Acknowledgment ☐ Oath/Affirmation ☐ Jurat ☐ Other/See Notes Fee $_____ Travel_____

Name (print)	Document type /Doc. name	Witness Name (print)	Date and Time Notarized
			_____ ___ _____ am / pm
Phone # / E-mail	Date of document	Witness Phone # / E-mail	Print of Right Thumb
Address	Satisfactory evidence of ID ☐ Driver's license ☐ Known Personally ☐ Credible Witness(es) ☐ Passport ☐ I.D. Card ☐ See Notes	Witness Address	
☐ ID. Issued by ☐ I.D. Number	☐ Expiration Date ☐ Issue Date	Notes	
Signer Signature		Witness Signature	

NOTARY PUBLIC JOURNAL – LARGE ENTRIES | 39

73
Service: ☐ Acknowledgment ☐ Oath/Affirmation ☐ Jurat ☐ Other/See Notes   Fee $_____   Travel_____

Name (print)	Document type /Doc. name	Witness Name (print)	Date and Time Notarized _____ ___ _____ am / pm
Phone # / E-mail	Date of document	Witness Phone # / E-mail	Print of Right Thumb
Address	Satisfactory evidence of ID ☐ Driver's license ☐ Known Personally ☐ Credible Witness(es) ☐ Passport ☐ I.D. Card ☐ See Notes	Witness Address	
☐ ID. Issued by ☐ I.D. Number	☐ Expiration Date ☐ Issue Date	Notes	
Signer Signature		Witness Signature	

74
Service: ☐ Acknowledgment ☐ Oath/Affirmation ☐ Jurat ☐ Other/See Notes   Fee $_____   Travel_____

Name (print)	Document type /Doc. name	Witness Name (print)	Date and Time Notarized _____ ___ _____ am / pm
Phone # / E-mail	Date of document	Witness Phone # / E-mail	Print of Right Thumb
Address	Satisfactory evidence of ID ☐ Driver's license ☐ Known Personally ☐ Credible Witness(es) ☐ Passport ☐ I.D. Card ☐ See Notes	Witness Address	
☐ ID. Issued by ☐ I.D. Number	☐ Expiration Date ☐ Issue Date	Notes	
Signer Signature		Witness Signature	

NOTARY PUBLIC JOURNAL – LARGE ENTRIES

75
Service: ☐ Acknowledgment   ☐ Oath/Affirmation   ☐ Jurat   ☐ Other/See Notes   Fee $_____   Travel_____

Name (print)	Document type /Doc. name	Witness Name (print)	Date and Time Notarized _____ ___ _____ am / pm
Phone # / E-mail	Date of document	Witness Phone # / E-mail	Print of Right Thumb
Address	Satisfactory evidence of ID ☐ Driver's license ☐ Known Personally ☐ Credible Witness(es) ☐ Passport ☐ I.D. Card ☐ See Notes	Witness Address	
☐ ID. Issued by ☐ I.D. Number	☐ Expiration Date ☐ Issue Date	Notes	
Signer Signature		Witness Signature	

76
Service: ☐ Acknowledgment   ☐ Oath/Affirmation   ☐ Jurat   ☐ Other/See Notes   Fee $_____   Travel_____

Name (print)	Document type /Doc. name	Witness Name (print)	Date and Time Notarized _____ ___ _____ am / pm
Phone # / E-mail	Date of document	Witness Phone # / E-mail	Print of Right Thumb
Address	Satisfactory evidence of ID ☐ Driver's license ☐ Known Personally ☐ Credible Witness(es) ☐ Passport ☐ I.D. Card ☐ See Notes	Witness Address	
☐ ID. Issued by ☐ I.D. Number	☐ Expiration Date ☐ Issue Date	Notes	
Signer Signature		Witness Signature	

NOTARY PUBLIC JOURNAL – LARGE ENTRIES | 41

77

Service: ☐ Acknowledgment ☐ Oath/Affirmation ☐ Jurat ☐ Other/See Notes   Fee $_____   Travel_____

Name (print)	Document type /Doc. name	Witness Name (print)	Date and Time Notarized _____ ___ _____ am / pm
Phone # / E-mail	Date of document	Witness Phone # / E-mail	Print of Right Thumb
Address	Satisfactory evidence of ID ☐ Driver's license ☐ Known Personally ☐ Credible Witness(es) ☐ Passport ☐ I.D. Card ☐ See Notes	Witness Address	
☐ ID. Issued by ☐ I.D. Number	☐ Expiration Date ☐ Issue Date	Notes	
Signer Signature		Witness Signature	

78

Service: ☐ Acknowledgment ☐ Oath/Affirmation ☐ Jurat ☐ Other/See Notes   Fee $_____   Travel_____

Name (print)	Document type /Doc. name	Witness Name (print)	Date and Time Notarized _____ ___ _____ am / pm
Phone # / E-mail	Date of document	Witness Phone # / E-mail	Print of Right Thumb
Address	Satisfactory evidence of ID ☐ Driver's license ☐ Known Personally ☐ Credible Witness(es) ☐ Passport ☐ I.D. Card ☐ See Notes	Witness Address	
☐ ID. Issued by ☐ I.D. Number	☐ Expiration Date ☐ Issue Date	Notes	
Signer Signature		Witness Signature	

42 NOTARY PUBLIC JOURNAL – LARGE ENTRIES

79
Service: ☐ Acknowledgment ☐ Oath/Affirmation ☐ Jurat ☐ Other/See Notes Fee $_____ Travel_____

Name (print)	Document type /Doc. name	Witness Name (print)	Date and Time Notarized _____ ___ _____ am / pm
Phone # / E-mail	Date of document	Witness Phone # / E-mail	Print of Right Thumb
Address	Satisfactory evidence of ID ☐ Driver's license ☐ Known Personally ☐ Credible Witness(es) ☐ Passport ☐ I.D. Card ☐ See Notes	Witness Address	
☐ ID. Issued by ☐ I.D. Number	☐ Expiration Date ☐ Issue Date	Notes	
Signer Signature		Witness Signature	

80
Service: ☐ Acknowledgment ☐ Oath/Affirmation ☐ Jurat ☐ Other/See Notes Fee $_____ Travel_____

Name (print)	Document type /Doc. name	Witness Name (print)	Date and Time Notarized _____ ___ _____ am / pm
Phone # / E-mail	Date of document	Witness Phone # / E-mail	Print of Right Thumb
Address	Satisfactory evidence of ID ☐ Driver's license ☐ Known Personally ☐ Credible Witness(es) ☐ Passport ☐ I.D. Card ☐ See Notes	Witness Address	
☐ ID. Issued by ☐ I.D. Number	☐ Expiration Date ☐ Issue Date	Notes	
Signer Signature		Witness Signature	

NOTARY PUBLIC JOURNAL – LARGE ENTRIES | 43

81

Service: ☐ Acknowledgment ☐ Oath/Affirmation ☐ Jurat ☐ Other/See Notes   Fee $_____ Travel_____

Name (print)	Document type /Doc. name	Witness Name (print)	Date and Time Notarized _____ ___ _____ am / pm
Phone # / E-mail	Date of document	Witness Phone # / E-mail	Print of Right Thumb
Address	Satisfactory evidence of ID ☐ Driver's license ☐ Known Personally ☐ Credible Witness(es) ☐ Passport ☐ I.D. Card ☐ See Notes	Witness Address	
☐ ID. Issued by ☐ I.D. Number	☐ Expiration Date ☐ Issue Date	Notes	
Signer Signature		Witness Signature	

82

Service: ☐ Acknowledgment ☐ Oath/Affirmation ☐ Jurat ☐ Other/See Notes   Fee $_____ Travel_____

Name (print)	Document type /Doc. name	Witness Name (print)	Date and Time Notarized _____ ___ _____ am / pm
Phone # / E-mail	Date of document	Witness Phone # / E-mail	Print of Right Thumb
Address	Satisfactory evidence of ID ☐ Driver's license ☐ Known Personally ☐ Credible Witness(es) ☐ Passport ☐ I.D. Card ☐ See Notes	Witness Address	
☐ ID. Issued by ☐ I.D. Number	☐ Expiration Date ☐ Issue Date	Notes	
Signer Signature		Witness Signature	

44 | **NOTARY PUBLIC JOURNAL – LARGE ENTRIES**

83

Service: ☐ Acknowledgment ☐ Oath/Affirmation ☐ Jurat ☐ Other/See Notes   Fee $_____   Travel_____

Name (print)	Document type /Doc. name	Witness Name (print)	Date and Time Notarized _____ ___ _____ am / pm
Phone # / E-mail	Date of document	Witness Phone # / E-mail	Print of Right Thumb
Address	Satisfactory evidence of ID ☐ Driver's license ☐ Known Personally ☐ Credible Witness(es) ☐ Passport ☐ I.D. Card ☐ See Notes	Witness Address	
☐ ID. Issued by ☐ I.D. Number	☐ Expiration Date ☐ Issue Date	Notes	
Signer Signature		Witness Signature	

84

Service: ☐ Acknowledgment ☐ Oath/Affirmation ☐ Jurat ☐ Other/See Notes   Fee $_____   Travel_____

Name (print)	Document type /Doc. name	Witness Name (print)	Date and Time Notarized _____ ___ _____ am / pm
Phone # / E-mail	Date of document	Witness Phone # / E-mail	Print of Right Thumb
Address	Satisfactory evidence of ID ☐ Driver's license ☐ Known Personally ☐ Credible Witness(es) ☐ Passport ☐ I.D. Card ☐ See Notes	Witness Address	
☐ ID. Issued by ☐ I.D. Number	☐ Expiration Date ☐ Issue Date	Notes	
Signer Signature		Witness Signature	

NOTARY PUBLIC JOURNAL – LARGE ENTRIES   45

85

Service: ☐ Acknowledgment ☐ Oath/Affirmation ☐ Jurat ☐ Other/See Notes   Fee $_____   Travel_____

Name (print)	Document type /Doc. name	Witness Name (print)	Date and Time Notarized _____ ___ _____ am / pm
Phone # / E-mail	Date of document	Witness Phone # / E-mail	Print of Right Thumb
Address	Satisfactory evidence of ID ☐ Driver's license ☐ Known Personally ☐ Credible Witness(es) ☐ Passport ☐ I.D. Card ☐ See Notes	Witness Address	
☐ ID. Issued by ☐ I.D. Number	☐ Expiration Date ☐ Issue Date	Notes	
Signer Signature		Witness Signature	

86

Service: ☐ Acknowledgment ☐ Oath/Affirmation ☐ Jurat ☐ Other/See Notes   Fee $_____   Travel_____

Name (print)	Document type /Doc. name	Witness Name (print)	Date and Time Notarized _____ ___ _____ am / pm
Phone # / E-mail	Date of document	Witness Phone # / E-mail	Print of Right Thumb
Address	Satisfactory evidence of ID ☐ Driver's license ☐ Known Personally ☐ Credible Witness(es) ☐ Passport ☐ I.D. Card ☐ See Notes	Witness Address	
☐ ID. Issued by ☐ I.D. Number	☐ Expiration Date ☐ Issue Date	Notes	
Signer Signature		Witness Signature	

46 NOTARY PUBLIC JOURNAL – LARGE ENTRIES

87

Service: ☐ Acknowledgment ☐ Oath/Affirmation ☐ Jurat ☐ Other/See Notes   Fee $_____   Travel_____

Name (print)	Document type /Doc. name	Witness Name (print)	Date and Time Notarized ____ ___ _____ am / pm
Phone # / E-mail	Date of document	Witness Phone # / E-mail	Print of Right Thumb
Address	Satisfactory evidence of ID ☐ Driver's license ☐ Known Personally ☐ Credible Witness(es) ☐ Passport ☐ I.D. Card ☐ See Notes	Witness Address	
☐ ID. Issued by ☐ I.D. Number	☐ Expiration Date ☐ Issue Date	Notes	
Signer Signature		Witness Signature	

88

Service: ☐ Acknowledgment ☐ Oath/Affirmation ☐ Jurat ☐ Other/See Notes   Fee $_____   Travel_____

Name (print)	Document type /Doc. name	Witness Name (print)	Date and Time Notarized ____ ___ _____ am / pm
Phone # / E-mail	Date of document	Witness Phone # / E-mail	Print of Right Thumb
Address	Satisfactory evidence of ID ☐ Driver's license ☐ Known Personally ☐ Credible Witness(es) ☐ Passport ☐ I.D. Card ☐ See Notes	Witness Address	
☐ ID. Issued by ☐ I.D. Number	☐ Expiration Date ☐ Issue Date	Notes	
Signer Signature		Witness Signature	

NOTARY PUBLIC JOURNAL – LARGE ENTRIES

89

Service: ☐ Acknowledgment ☐ Oath/Affirmation ☐ Jurat ☐ Other/See Notes Fee $_____ Travel_____

Name (print)	Document type /Doc. name	Witness Name (print)	Date and Time Notarized _____ __ _____ am / pm
Phone # / E-mail	Date of document	Witness Phone # / E-mail	Print of Right Thumb
Address	Satisfactory evidence of ID ☐ Driver's license ☐ Known Personally ☐ Credible Witness(es) ☐ Passport ☐ I.D. Card ☐ See Notes	Witness Address	
☐ ID. Issued by ☐ I.D. Number	☐ Expiration Date ☐ Issue Date	Notes	
Signer Signature		Witness Signature	

90

Service: ☐ Acknowledgment ☐ Oath/Affirmation ☐ Jurat ☐ Other/See Notes Fee $_____ Travel_____

Name (print)	Document type /Doc. name	Witness Name (print)	Date and Time Notarized _____ __ _____ am / pm
Phone # / E-mail	Date of document	Witness Phone # / E-mail	Print of Right Thumb
Address	Satisfactory evidence of ID ☐ Driver's license ☐ Known Personally ☐ Credible Witness(es) ☐ Passport ☐ I.D. Card ☐ See Notes	Witness Address	
☐ ID. Issued by ☐ I.D. Number	☐ Expiration Date ☐ Issue Date	Notes	
Signer Signature		Witness Signature	

48 NOTARY PUBLIC JOURNAL – LARGE ENTRIES

91
Service: ☐ Acknowledgment ☐ Oath/Affirmation ☐ Jurat ☐ Other/See Notes   Fee $_____   Travel_____

Name (print)	Document type /Doc. name	Witness Name (print)	Date and Time Notarized _____ ___ _____ am / pm
Phone # / E-mail	Date of document	Witness Phone # / E-mail	Print of Right Thumb
Address	Satisfactory evidence of ID ☐ Driver's license ☐ Known Personally ☐ Credible Witness(es) ☐ Passport ☐ I.D. Card ☐ See Notes	Witness Address	
☐ ID. Issued by ☐ I.D. Number	☐ Expiration Date ☐ Issue Date	Notes	
Signer Signature		Witness Signature	

92
Service: ☐ Acknowledgment ☐ Oath/Affirmation ☐ Jurat ☐ Other/See Notes   Fee $_____   Travel_____

Name (print)	Document type /Doc. name	Witness Name (print)	Date and Time Notarized _____ ___ _____ am / pm
Phone # / E-mail	Date of document	Witness Phone # / E-mail	Print of Right Thumb
Address	Satisfactory evidence of ID ☐ Driver's license ☐ Known Personally ☐ Credible Witness(es) ☐ Passport ☐ I.D. Card ☐ See Notes	Witness Address	
☐ ID. Issued by ☐ I.D. Number	☐ Expiration Date ☐ Issue Date	Notes	
Signer Signature		Witness Signature	

NOTARY PUBLIC JOURNAL – LARGE ENTRIES — 49

93

Service: ☐ Acknowledgment ☐ Oath/Affirmation ☐ Jurat ☐ Other/See Notes   Fee $_____   Travel_____

Name (print)	Document type /Doc. name	Witness Name (print)	Date and Time Notarized _____ __ _____ am / pm
Phone # / E-mail	Date of document	Witness Phone # / E-mail	Print of Right Thumb
Address	Satisfactory evidence of ID ☐ Driver's license ☐ Known Personally ☐ Credible Witness(es) ☐ Passport ☐ I.D. Card ☐ See Notes	Witness Address	
☐ ID. Issued by ☐ I.D. Number	☐ Expiration Date ☐ Issue Date	Notes	
Signer Signature		Witness Signature	

94

Service: ☐ Acknowledgment ☐ Oath/Affirmation ☐ Jurat ☐ Other/See Notes   Fee $_____   Travel_____

Name (print)	Document type /Doc. name	Witness Name (print)	Date and Time Notarized _____ __ _____ am / pm
Phone # / E-mail	Date of document	Witness Phone # / E-mail	Print of Right Thumb
Address	Satisfactory evidence of ID ☐ Driver's license ☐ Known Personally ☐ Credible Witness(es) ☐ Passport ☐ I.D. Card ☐ See Notes	Witness Address	
☐ ID. Issued by ☐ I.D. Number	☐ Expiration Date ☐ Issue Date	Notes	
Signer Signature		Witness Signature	

50 | NOTARY PUBLIC JOURNAL – LARGE ENTRIES

95

Service: ☐ Acknowledgment ☐ Oath/Affirmation ☐ Jurat ☐ Other/See Notes Fee $_____ Travel_____

Name (print)	Document type /Doc. name	Witness Name (print)	Date and Time Notarized _____ ___ _____ am / pm
Phone # / E-mail	Date of document	Witness Phone # / E-mail	Print of Right Thumb
Address	Satisfactory evidence of ID ☐ Driver's license ☐ Known Personally ☐ Credible Witness(es) ☐ Passport ☐ I.D. Card ☐ See Notes	Witness Address	
☐ ID. Issued by ☐ I.D. Number	☐ Expiration Date ☐ Issue Date	Notes	
Signer Signature		Witness Signature	

96

Service: ☐ Acknowledgment ☐ Oath/Affirmation ☐ Jurat ☐ Other/See Notes Fee $_____ Travel_____

Name (print)	Document type /Doc. name	Witness Name (print)	Date and Time Notarized _____ ___ _____ am / pm
Phone # / E-mail	Date of document	Witness Phone # / E-mail	Print of Right Thumb
Address	Satisfactory evidence of ID ☐ Driver's license ☐ Known Personally ☐ Credible Witness(es) ☐ Passport ☐ I.D. Card ☐ See Notes	Witness Address	
☐ ID. Issued by ☐ I.D. Number	☐ Expiration Date ☐ Issue Date	Notes	
Signer Signature		Witness Signature	

NOTARY PUBLIC JOURNAL – LARGE ENTRIES | 51

97 Service: ☐ Acknowledgment ☐ Oath/Affirmation ☐ Jurat ☐ Other/See Notes Fee $_____ Travel_____

Name (print)	Document type /Doc. name	Witness Name (print)	Date and Time Notarized _____ ___ _____ am / pm
Phone # / E-mail	Date of document	Witness Phone # / E-mail	Print of Right Thumb
Address	Satisfactory evidence of ID ☐ Driver's license ☐ Known Personally ☐ Credible Witness(es) ☐ Passport ☐ I.D. Card ☐ See Notes	Witness Address	
☐ ID. Issued by ☐ I.D. Number	☐ Expiration Date ☐ Issue Date	Notes	
Signer Signature		Witness Signature	

98 Service: ☐ Acknowledgment ☐ Oath/Affirmation ☐ Jurat ☐ Other/See Notes Fee $_____ Travel_____

Name (print)	Document type /Doc. name	Witness Name (print)	Date and Time Notarized _____ ___ _____ am / pm
Phone # / E-mail	Date of document	Witness Phone # / E-mail	Print of Right Thumb
Address	Satisfactory evidence of ID ☐ Driver's license ☐ Known Personally ☐ Credible Witness(es) ☐ Passport ☐ I.D. Card ☐ See Notes	Witness Address	
☐ ID. Issued by ☐ I.D. Number	☐ Expiration Date ☐ Issue Date	Notes	
Signer Signature		Witness Signature	

NOTARY PUBLIC JOURNAL – LARGE ENTRIES

99

Service: ☐ Acknowledgment ☐ Oath/Affirmation ☐ Jurat ☐ Other/See Notes   Fee $_____   Travel_____

Name (print)	Document type /Doc. name	Witness Name (print)	Date and Time Notarized _____ ___ _____ am / pm
Phone # / E-mail	Date of document	Witness Phone # / E-mail	Print of Right Thumb
Address	Satisfactory evidence of ID ☐ Driver's license ☐ Known Personally ☐ Credible Witness(es) ☐ Passport ☐ I.D. Card ☐ See Notes	Witness Address	
☐ ID. Issued by ☐ I.D. Number	☐ Expiration Date ☐ Issue Date	Notes	
Signer Signature		Witness Signature	

100

Service: ☐ Acknowledgment ☐ Oath/Affirmation ☐ Jurat ☐ Other/See Notes   Fee $_____   Travel_____

Name (print)	Document type /Doc. name	Witness Name (print)	Date and Time Notarized _____ ___ _____ am / pm
Phone # / E-mail	Date of document	Witness Phone # / E-mail	Print of Right Thumb
Address	Satisfactory evidence of ID ☐ Driver's license ☐ Known Personally ☐ Credible Witness(es) ☐ Passport ☐ I.D. Card ☐ See Notes	Witness Address	
☐ ID. Issued by ☐ I.D. Number	☐ Expiration Date ☐ Issue Date	Notes	
Signer Signature		Witness Signature	

NOTARY PUBLIC JOURNAL – LARGE ENTRIES | 53

101
Service: ☐ Acknowledgment ☐ Oath/Affirmation ☐ Jurat ☐ Other/See Notes   Fee $_____   Travel_____

Name (print)	Document type /Doc. name	Witness Name (print)	Date and Time Notarized _____ ___ _____ am / pm
Phone # / E-mail	Date of document	Witness Phone # / E-mail	Print of Right Thumb
Address	Satisfactory evidence of ID ☐ Driver's license ☐ Known Personally ☐ Credible Witness(es) ☐ Passport ☐ I.D. Card ☐ See Notes	Witness Address	
☐ ID. Issued by ☐ I.D. Number	☐ Expiration Date ☐ Issue Date	Notes	
Signer Signature		Witness Signature	

102
Service: ☐ Acknowledgment ☐ Oath/Affirmation ☐ Jurat ☐ Other/See Notes   Fee $_____   Travel_____

Name (print)	Document type /Doc. name	Witness Name (print)	Date and Time Notarized _____ ___ _____ am / pm
Phone # / E-mail	Date of document	Witness Phone # / E-mail	Print of Right Thumb
Address	Satisfactory evidence of ID ☐ Driver's license ☐ Known Personally ☐ Credible Witness(es) ☐ Passport ☐ I.D. Card ☐ See Notes	Witness Address	
☐ ID. Issued by ☐ I.D. Number	☐ Expiration Date ☐ Issue Date	Notes	
Signer Signature		Witness Signature	

54 NOTARY PUBLIC JOURNAL – LARGE ENTRIES

103 Service: ☐ Acknowledgment ☐ Oath/Affirmation ☐ Jurat ☐ Other/See Notes   Fee $_____   Travel_____

Name (print)	Document type /Doc. name	Witness Name (print)	Date and Time Notarized _____ ___ _____ am / pm
Phone # / E-mail	Date of document	Witness Phone # / E-mail	Print of Right Thumb
Address	Satisfactory evidence of ID ☐ Driver's license ☐ Known Personally ☐ Credible Witness(es) ☐ Passport ☐ I.D. Card ☐ See Notes	Witness Address	
☐ ID. Issued by ☐ I.D. Number	☐ Expiration Date ☐ Issue Date	Notes	
Signer Signature		Witness Signature	

104 Service: ☐ Acknowledgment ☐ Oath/Affirmation ☐ Jurat ☐ Other/See Notes   Fee $_____   Travel_____

Name (print)	Document type /Doc. name	Witness Name (print)	Date and Time Notarized _____ ___ _____ am / pm
Phone # / E-mail	Date of document	Witness Phone # / E-mail	Print of Right Thumb
Address	Satisfactory evidence of ID ☐ Driver's license ☐ Known Personally ☐ Credible Witness(es) ☐ Passport ☐ I.D. Card ☐ See Notes	Witness Address	
☐ ID. Issued by ☐ I.D. Number	☐ Expiration Date ☐ Issue Date	Notes	
Signer Signature		Witness Signature	

NOTARY PUBLIC JOURNAL – LARGE ENTRIES | 55

105
Service: ☐ Acknowledgment ☐ Oath/Affirmation ☐ Jurat ☐ Other/See Notes   Fee $_____   Travel_____

Name (print)	Document type /Doc. name	Witness Name (print)	Date and Time Notarized _____ ___ _____ am / pm
Phone # / E-mail	Date of document	Witness Phone # / E-mail	Print of Right Thumb
Address	Satisfactory evidence of ID ☐ Driver's license ☐ Known Personally ☐ Credible Witness(es) ☐ Passport ☐ I.D. Card ☐ See Notes	Witness Address	
☐ ID. Issued by ☐ I.D. Number	☐ Expiration Date ☐ Issue Date	Notes	
Signer Signature		Witness Signature	

106
Service: ☐ Acknowledgment ☐ Oath/Affirmation ☐ Jurat ☐ Other/See Notes   Fee $_____   Travel_____

Name (print)	Document type /Doc. name	Witness Name (print)	Date and Time Notarized _____ ___ _____ am / pm
Phone # / E-mail	Date of document	Witness Phone # / E-mail	Print of Right Thumb
Address	Satisfactory evidence of ID ☐ Driver's license ☐ Known Personally ☐ Credible Witness(es) ☐ Passport ☐ I.D. Card ☐ See Notes	Witness Address	
☐ ID. Issued by ☐ I.D. Number	☐ Expiration Date ☐ Issue Date	Notes	
Signer Signature		Witness Signature	

NOTARY PUBLIC JOURNAL – LARGE ENTRIES

107
Service: ☐ Acknowledgment ☐ Oath/Affirmation ☐ Jurat ☐ Other/See Notes   Fee $_____   Travel_____

Name (print)	Document type /Doc. name	Witness Name (print)	Date and Time Notarized
			_____ ___ _____ am / pm
Phone # / E-mail	Date of document	Witness Phone # / E-mail	Print of Right Thumb
Address	Satisfactory evidence of ID ☐ Driver's license ☐ Known Personally ☐ Credible Witness(es) ☐ Passport ☐ I.D. Card ☐ See Notes	Witness Address	
☐ ID. Issued by ☐ I.D. Number	☐ Expiration Date ☐ Issue Date	Notes	
Signer Signature		Witness Signature	

108
Service: ☐ Acknowledgment ☐ Oath/Affirmation ☐ Jurat ☐ Other/See Notes   Fee $_____   Travel_____

Name (print)	Document type /Doc. name	Witness Name (print)	Date and Time Notarized
			_____ ___ _____ am / pm
Phone # / E-mail	Date of document	Witness Phone # / E-mail	Print of Right Thumb
Address	Satisfactory evidence of ID ☐ Driver's license ☐ Known Personally ☐ Credible Witness(es) ☐ Passport ☐ I.D. Card ☐ See Notes	Witness Address	
☐ ID. Issued by ☐ I.D. Number	☐ Expiration Date ☐ Issue Date	Notes	
Signer Signature		Witness Signature	

NOTARY PUBLIC JOURNAL – LARGE ENTRIES

109

Service: ☐ Acknowledgment ☐ Oath/Affirmation ☐ Jurat ☐ Other/See Notes   Fee $_____   Travel_____

Name (print)	Document type /Doc. name	Witness Name (print)	Date and Time Notarized _____ ___ _____ am / pm
Phone # / E-mail	Date of document	Witness Phone # / E-mail	Print of Right Thumb
Address	Satisfactory evidence of ID ☐ Driver's license ☐ Known Personally ☐ Credible Witness(es) ☐ Passport ☐ I.D. Card ☐ See Notes	Witness Address	
☐ ID. Issued by ☐ I.D. Number	☐ Expiration Date ☐ Issue Date	Notes	
Signer Signature		Witness Signature	

110

Service: ☐ Acknowledgment ☐ Oath/Affirmation ☐ Jurat ☐ Other/See Notes   Fee $_____   Travel_____

Name (print)	Document type /Doc. name	Witness Name (print)	Date and Time Notarized _____ ___ _____ am / pm
Phone # / E-mail	Date of document	Witness Phone # / E-mail	Print of Right Thumb
Address	Satisfactory evidence of ID ☐ Driver's license ☐ Known Personally ☐ Credible Witness(es) ☐ Passport ☐ I.D. Card ☐ See Notes	Witness Address	
☐ ID. Issued by ☐ I.D. Number	☐ Expiration Date ☐ Issue Date	Notes	
Signer Signature		Witness Signature	

NOTARY PUBLIC JOURNAL – LARGE ENTRIES

111

Service: ☐ Acknowledgment ☐ Oath/Affirmation ☐ Jurat ☐ Other/See Notes   Fee $_____   Travel_____

Name (print)	Document type /Doc. name	Witness Name (print)	Date and Time Notarized _____ ___ _____ am / pm
Phone # / E-mail	Date of document	Witness Phone # / E-mail	Print of Right Thumb
Address	Satisfactory evidence of ID ☐ Driver's license ☐ Known Personally ☐ Credible Witness(es) ☐ Passport ☐ I.D. Card ☐ See Notes	Witness Address	
☐ ID. Issued by ☐ I.D. Number	☐ Expiration Date ☐ Issue Date	Notes	
Signer Signature		Witness Signature	

112

Service: ☐ Acknowledgment ☐ Oath/Affirmation ☐ Jurat ☐ Other/See Notes   Fee $_____   Travel_____

Name (print)	Document type /Doc. name	Witness Name (print)	Date and Time Notarized _____ ___ _____ am / pm
Phone # / E-mail	Date of document	Witness Phone # / E-mail	Print of Right Thumb
Address	Satisfactory evidence of ID ☐ Driver's license ☐ Known Personally ☐ Credible Witness(es) ☐ Passport ☐ I.D. Card ☐ See Notes	Witness Address	
☐ ID. Issued by ☐ I.D. Number	☐ Expiration Date ☐ Issue Date	Notes	
Signer Signature		Witness Signature	

113 Service: ☐ Acknowledgment ☐ Oath/Affirmation ☐ Jurat ☐ Other/See Notes   Fee $_____   Travel_____

Name (print)	Document type /Doc. name	Witness Name (print)	Date and Time Notarized _____ ___ _____ am / pm
Phone # / E-mail	Date of document	Witness Phone # / E-mail	Print of Right Thumb
Address	Satisfactory evidence of ID ☐ Driver's license ☐ Known Personally ☐ Credible Witness(es) ☐ Passport ☐ I.D. Card ☐ See Notes	Witness Address	
☐ ID. Issued by ☐ I.D. Number	☐ Expiration Date ☐ Issue Date	Notes	
Signer Signature		Witness Signature	

114 Service: ☐ Acknowledgment ☐ Oath/Affirmation ☐ Jurat ☐ Other/See Notes   Fee $_____   Travel_____

Name (print)	Document type /Doc. name	Witness Name (print)	Date and Time Notarized _____ ___ _____ am / pm
Phone # / E-mail	Date of document	Witness Phone # / E-mail	Print of Right Thumb
Address	Satisfactory evidence of ID ☐ Driver's license ☐ Known Personally ☐ Credible Witness(es) ☐ Passport ☐ I.D. Card ☐ See Notes	Witness Address	
☐ ID. Issued by ☐ I.D. Number	☐ Expiration Date ☐ Issue Date	Notes	
Signer Signature		Witness Signature	

NOTARY PUBLIC JOURNAL – LARGE ENTRIES

115 Service: ☐ Acknowledgment ☐ Oath/Affirmation ☐ Jurat ☐ Other/See Notes   Fee $_____   Travel_____

Name (print)	Document type /Doc. name	Witness Name (print)	Date and Time Notarized _____ ___ _____ am / pm
Phone # / E-mail	Date of document	Witness Phone # / E-mail	Print of Right Thumb
Address	Satisfactory evidence of ID ☐ Driver's license ☐ Known Personally ☐ Credible Witness(es) ☐ Passport ☐ I.D. Card ☐ See Notes	Witness Address	
☐ ID. Issued by ☐ I.D. Number	☐ Expiration Date ☐ Issue Date	Notes	
Signer Signature		Witness Signature	

116 Service: ☐ Acknowledgment ☐ Oath/Affirmation ☐ Jurat ☐ Other/See Notes   Fee $_____   Travel_____

Name (print)	Document type /Doc. name	Witness Name (print)	Date and Time Notarized _____ ___ _____ am / pm
Phone # / E-mail	Date of document	Witness Phone # / E-mail	Print of Right Thumb
Address	Satisfactory evidence of ID ☐ Driver's license ☐ Known Personally ☐ Credible Witness(es) ☐ Passport ☐ I.D. Card ☐ See Notes	Witness Address	
☐ ID. Issued by ☐ I.D. Number	☐ Expiration Date ☐ Issue Date	Notes	
Signer Signature		Witness Signature	

NOTARY PUBLIC JOURNAL – LARGE ENTRIES 61

117
Service: ☐ Acknowledgment ☐ Oath/Affirmation ☐ Jurat ☐ Other/See Notes   Fee $_____   Travel_____

Name (print)	Document type /Doc. name	Witness Name (print)	Date and Time Notarized _____ ___ _____ am / pm
Phone # / E-mail	Date of document	Witness Phone # / E-mail	Print of Right Thumb
Address	Satisfactory evidence of ID ☐ Driver's license ☐ Known Personally ☐ Credible Witness(es) ☐ Passport ☐ I.D. Card ☐ See Notes	Witness Address	
☐ ID. Issued by ☐ I.D. Number	☐ Expiration Date ☐ Issue Date	Notes	
Signer Signature		Witness Signature	

118
Service: ☐ Acknowledgment ☐ Oath/Affirmation ☐ Jurat ☐ Other/See Notes   Fee $_____   Travel_____

Name (print)	Document type /Doc. name	Witness Name (print)	Date and Time Notarized _____ ___ _____ am / pm
Phone # / E-mail	Date of document	Witness Phone # / E-mail	Print of Right Thumb
Address	Satisfactory evidence of ID ☐ Driver's license ☐ Known Personally ☐ Credible Witness(es) ☐ Passport ☐ I.D. Card ☐ See Notes	Witness Address	
☐ ID. Issued by ☐ I.D. Number	☐ Expiration Date ☐ Issue Date	Notes	
Signer Signature		Witness Signature	

NOTARY PUBLIC JOURNAL – LARGE ENTRIES

119

Service: ☐ Acknowledgment ☐ Oath/Affirmation ☐ Jurat ☐ Other/See Notes Fee $_____ Travel_____

Name (print)	Document type /Doc. name	Witness Name (print)	Date and Time Notarized _____ ___ _____ am / pm
Phone # / E-mail	Date of document	Witness Phone # / E-mail	Print of Right Thumb
Address	Satisfactory evidence of ID ☐ Driver's license ☐ Known Personally ☐ Credible Witness(es) ☐ Passport ☐ I.D. Card ☐ See Notes	Witness Address	
☐ ID. Issued by .... ☐ I.D. Number	☐ Expiration Date .... ☐ Issue Date	Notes	
Signer Signature		Witness Signature	

120

Service: ☐ Acknowledgment ☐ Oath/Affirmation ☐ Jurat ☐ Other/See Notes Fee $_____ Travel_____

Name (print)	Document type /Doc. name	Witness Name (print)	Date and Time Notarized _____ ___ _____ am / pm
Phone # / E-mail	Date of document	Witness Phone # / E-mail	Print of Right Thumb
Address	Satisfactory evidence of ID ☐ Driver's license ☐ Known Personally ☐ Credible Witness(es) ☐ Passport ☐ I.D. Card ☐ See Notes	Witness Address	
☐ ID. Issued by .... ☐ I.D. Number	☐ Expiration Date .... ☐ Issue Date	Notes	
Signer Signature		Witness Signature	

NOTARY PUBLIC JOURNAL – LARGE ENTRIES 63

121
Service: ☐ Acknowledgment ☐ Oath/Affirmation ☐ Jurat ☐ Other/See Notes   Fee $_____   Travel_____

Name (print)	Document type /Doc. name	Witness Name (print)	Date and Time Notarized _____ ___ _____ am / pm
Phone # / E-mail	Date of document	Witness Phone # / E-mail	Print of Right Thumb
Address	Satisfactory evidence of ID ☐ Driver's license ☐ Known Personally ☐ Credible Witness(es) ☐ Passport ☐ I.D. Card ☐ See Notes	Witness Address	
☐ ID. Issued by ☐ I.D. Number	☐ Expiration Date ☐ Issue Date	Notes	
Signer Signature		Witness Signature	

122
Service: ☐ Acknowledgment ☐ Oath/Affirmation ☐ Jurat ☐ Other/See Notes   Fee $_____   Travel_____

Name (print)	Document type /Doc. name	Witness Name (print)	Date and Time Notarized _____ ___ _____ am / pm
Phone # / E-mail	Date of document	Witness Phone # / E-mail	Print of Right Thumb
Address	Satisfactory evidence of ID ☐ Driver's license ☐ Known Personally ☐ Credible Witness(es) ☐ Passport ☐ I.D. Card ☐ See Notes	Witness Address	
☐ ID. Issued by ☐ I.D. Number	☐ Expiration Date ☐ Issue Date	Notes	
Signer Signature		Witness Signature	

NOTARY PUBLIC JOURNAL – LARGE ENTRIES

123
Service: ☐ Acknowledgment ☐ Oath/Affirmation ☐ Jurat ☐ Other/See Notes   Fee $_____   Travel_____

Name (print)	Document type /Doc. name	Witness Name (print)	Date and Time Notarized _____ ___ _____ am / pm
Phone # / E-mail	Date of document	Witness Phone # / E-mail	Print of Right Thumb
Address	Satisfactory evidence of ID ☐ Driver's license ☐ Known Personally ☐ Credible Witness(es) ☐ Passport ☐ I.D. Card ☐ See Notes	Witness Address	
☐ ID. Issued by ☐ I.D. Number	☐ Expiration Date ☐ Issue Date	Notes	
Signer Signature		Witness Signature	

124
Service: ☐ Acknowledgment ☐ Oath/Affirmation ☐ Jurat ☐ Other/See Notes   Fee $_____   Travel_____

Name (print)	Document type /Doc. name	Witness Name (print)	Date and Time Notarized _____ ___ _____ am / pm
Phone # / E-mail	Date of document	Witness Phone # / E-mail	Print of Right Thumb
Address	Satisfactory evidence of ID ☐ Driver's license ☐ Known Personally ☐ Credible Witness(es) ☐ Passport ☐ I.D. Card ☐ See Notes	Witness Address	
☐ ID. Issued by ☐ I.D. Number	☐ Expiration Date ☐ Issue Date	Notes	
Signer Signature		Witness Signature	

NOTARY PUBLIC JOURNAL – LARGE ENTRIES | 65

125
Service: ☐ Acknowledgment ☐ Oath/Affirmation ☐ Jurat ☐ Other/See Notes Fee $_____ Travel_____

Name (print)	Document type /Doc. name	Witness Name (print)	Date and Time Notarized _____ ___ _____ am / pm
Phone # / E-mail	Date of document	Witness Phone # / E-mail	Print of Right Thumb
Address	Satisfactory evidence of ID ☐ Driver's license ☐ Known Personally ☐ Credible Witness(es) ☐ Passport ☐ I.D. Card ☐ See Notes	Witness Address	
☐ ID. Issued by ☐ I.D. Number	☐ Expiration Date ☐ Issue Date	Notes	
Signer Signature		Witness Signature	

126
Service: ☐ Acknowledgment ☐ Oath/Affirmation ☐ Jurat ☐ Other/See Notes Fee $_____ Travel_____

Name (print)	Document type /Doc. name	Witness Name (print)	Date and Time Notarized _____ ___ _____ am / pm
Phone # / E-mail	Date of document	Witness Phone # / E-mail	Print of Right Thumb
Address	Satisfactory evidence of ID ☐ Driver's license ☐ Known Personally ☐ Credible Witness(es) ☐ Passport ☐ I.D. Card ☐ See Notes	Witness Address	
☐ ID. Issued by ☐ I.D. Number	☐ Expiration Date ☐ Issue Date	Notes	
Signer Signature		Witness Signature	

NOTARY PUBLIC JOURNAL – LARGE ENTRIES

127

Service: ☐ Acknowledgment ☐ Oath/Affirmation ☐ Jurat ☐ Other/See Notes   Fee $_____   Travel_____

Name (print)	Document type /Doc. name	Witness Name (print)	Date and Time Notarized _____ ___ _____ am / pm
Phone # / E-mail	Date of document	Witness Phone # / E-mail	Print of Right Thumb
Address	Satisfactory evidence of ID ☐ Driver's license ☐ Known Personally ☐ Credible Witness(es) ☐ Passport ☐ I.D. Card ☐ See Notes	Witness Address	
☐ ID. Issued by ☐ I.D. Number	☐ Expiration Date ☐ Issue Date	Notes	
Signer Signature		Witness Signature	

128

Service: ☐ Acknowledgment ☐ Oath/Affirmation ☐ Jurat ☐ Other/See Notes   Fee $_____   Travel_____

Name (print)	Document type /Doc. name	Witness Name (print)	Date and Time Notarized _____ ___ _____ am / pm
Phone # / E-mail	Date of document	Witness Phone # / E-mail	Print of Right Thumb
Address	Satisfactory evidence of ID ☐ Driver's license ☐ Known Personally ☐ Credible Witness(es) ☐ Passport ☐ I.D. Card ☐ See Notes	Witness Address	
☐ ID. Issued by ☐ I.D. Number	☐ Expiration Date ☐ Issue Date	Notes	
Signer Signature		Witness Signature	

NOTARY PUBLIC JOURNAL – LARGE ENTRIES

129
Service: ☐ Acknowledgment ☐ Oath/Affirmation ☐ Jurat ☐ Other/See Notes Fee $_____ Travel_____

Name (print)	Document type /Doc. name	Witness Name (print)	Date and Time Notarized _____ ___ _____ am / pm
Phone # / E-mail	Date of document	Witness Phone # / E-mail	Print of Right Thumb
Address	Satisfactory evidence of ID ☐ Driver's license ☐ Known Personally ☐ Credible Witness(es) ☐ Passport ☐ I.D. Card ☐ See Notes	Witness Address	
☐ ID. Issued by ☐ I.D. Number	☐ Expiration Date ☐ Issue Date	Notes	
Signer Signature		Witness Signature	

130
Service: ☐ Acknowledgment ☐ Oath/Affirmation ☐ Jurat ☐ Other/See Notes Fee $_____ Travel_____

Name (print)	Document type /Doc. name	Witness Name (print)	Date and Time Notarized _____ ___ _____ am / pm
Phone # / E-mail	Date of document	Witness Phone # / E-mail	Print of Right Thumb
Address	Satisfactory evidence of ID ☐ Driver's license ☐ Known Personally ☐ Credible Witness(es) ☐ Passport ☐ I.D. Card ☐ See Notes	Witness Address	
☐ ID. Issued by ☐ I.D. Number	☐ Expiration Date ☐ Issue Date	Notes	
Signer Signature		Witness Signature	

131

Service: ☐ Acknowledgment ☐ Oath/Affirmation ☐ Jurat ☐ Other/See Notes   Fee $ _____   Travel _____

Name (print)	Document type /Doc. name	Witness Name (print)	Date and Time Notarized _____ ___ _____ am / pm
Phone # / E-mail	Date of document	Witness Phone # / E-mail	Print of Right Thumb
Address	Satisfactory evidence of ID ☐ Driver's license ☐ Known Personally ☐ Credible Witness(es) ☐ Passport ☐ I.D. Card ☐ See Notes	Witness Address	
☐ ID. Issued by .... ☐ I.D. Number	☐ Expiration Date .... ☐ Issue Date	Notes	
Signer Signature		Witness Signature	

132

Service: ☐ Acknowledgment ☐ Oath/Affirmation ☐ Jurat ☐ Other/See Notes   Fee $ _____   Travel _____

Name (print)	Document type /Doc. name	Witness Name (print)	Date and Time Notarized _____ ___ _____ am / pm
Phone # / E-mail	Date of document	Witness Phone # / E-mail	Print of Right Thumb
Address	Satisfactory evidence of ID ☐ Driver's license ☐ Known Personally ☐ Credible Witness(es) ☐ Passport ☐ I.D. Card ☐ See Notes	Witness Address	
☐ ID. Issued by .... ☐ I.D. Number	☐ Expiration Date .... ☐ Issue Date	Notes	
Signer Signature		Witness Signature	

NOTARY PUBLIC JOURNAL – LARGE ENTRIES 69

133

Service: ☐ Acknowledgment ☐ Oath/Affirmation ☐ Jurat ☐ Other/See Notes   Fee $_____   Travel_____

Name (print)	Document type /Doc. name	Witness Name (print)	Date and Time Notarized _____ ___ _____ am / pm
Phone # / E-mail	Date of document	Witness Phone # / E-mail	Print of Right Thumb
Address	Satisfactory evidence of ID ☐ Driver's license ☐ Known Personally ☐ Credible Witness(es) ☐ Passport ☐ I.D. Card ☐ See Notes	Witness Address	
☐ ID. Issued by ☐ I.D. Number	☐ Expiration Date ☐ Issue Date	Notes	
Signer Signature		Witness Signature	

134

Service: ☐ Acknowledgment ☐ Oath/Affirmation ☐ Jurat ☐ Other/See Notes   Fee $_____   Travel_____

Name (print)	Document type /Doc. name	Witness Name (print)	Date and Time Notarized _____ ___ _____ am / pm
Phone # / E-mail	Date of document	Witness Phone # / E-mail	Print of Right Thumb
Address	Satisfactory evidence of ID ☐ Driver's license ☐ Known Personally ☐ Credible Witness(es) ☐ Passport ☐ I.D. Card ☐ See Notes	Witness Address	
☐ ID. Issued by ☐ I.D. Number	☐ Expiration Date ☐ Issue Date	Notes	
Signer Signature		Witness Signature	

NOTARY PUBLIC JOURNAL – LARGE ENTRIES

135

Service: ☐ Acknowledgment ☐ Oath/Affirmation ☐ Jurat ☐ Other/See Notes Fee $_____ Travel_____

Name (print)	Document type /Doc. name	Witness Name (print)	Date and Time Notarized _____ ___ _____ am / pm
Phone # / E-mail	Date of document	Witness Phone # / E-mail	Print of Right Thumb
Address	Satisfactory evidence of ID ☐ Driver's license ☐ Known Personally ☐ Credible Witness(es) ☐ Passport ☐ I.D. Card ☐ See Notes	Witness Address	
☐ ID. Issued by ☐ I.D. Number	☐ Expiration Date ☐ Issue Date	Notes	
Signer Signature		Witness Signature	

136

Service: ☐ Acknowledgment ☐ Oath/Affirmation ☐ Jurat ☐ Other/See Notes Fee $_____ Travel_____

Name (print)	Document type /Doc. name	Witness Name (print)	Date and Time Notarized _____ ___ _____ am / pm
Phone # / E-mail	Date of document	Witness Phone # / E-mail	Print of Right Thumb
Address	Satisfactory evidence of ID ☐ Driver's license ☐ Known Personally ☐ Credible Witness(es) ☐ Passport ☐ I.D. Card ☐ See Notes	Witness Address	
☐ ID. Issued by ☐ I.D. Number	☐ Expiration Date ☐ Issue Date	Notes	
Signer Signature		Witness Signature	

NOTARY PUBLIC JOURNAL – LARGE ENTRIES | 71

137
Service: ☐ Acknowledgment ☐ Oath/Affirmation ☐ Jurat ☐ Other/See Notes   Fee $_____   Travel_____

Name (print)	Document type /Doc. name	Witness Name (print)	Date and Time Notarized _____ ___ _____ am / pm
Phone # / E-mail	Date of document	Witness Phone # / E-mail	Print of Right Thumb
Address	Satisfactory evidence of ID ☐ Driver's license ☐ Known Personally ☐ Credible Witness(es) ☐ Passport ☐ I.D. Card ☐ See Notes	Witness Address	
☐ ID. Issued by ☐ I.D. Number	☐ Expiration Date ☐ Issue Date	Notes	
Signer Signature		Witness Signature	

138
Service: ☐ Acknowledgment ☐ Oath/Affirmation ☐ Jurat ☐ Other/See Notes   Fee $_____   Travel_____

Name (print)	Document type /Doc. name	Witness Name (print)	Date and Time Notarized _____ ___ _____ am / pm
Phone # / E-mail	Date of document	Witness Phone # / E-mail	Print of Right Thumb
Address	Satisfactory evidence of ID ☐ Driver's license ☐ Known Personally ☐ Credible Witness(es) ☐ Passport ☐ I.D. Card ☐ See Notes	Witness Address	
☐ ID. Issued by ☐ I.D. Number	☐ Expiration Date ☐ Issue Date	Notes	
Signer Signature		Witness Signature	

NOTARY PUBLIC JOURNAL – LARGE ENTRIES

139
Service: ☐ Acknowledgment ☐ Oath/Affirmation ☐ Jurat ☐ Other/See Notes   Fee $_____ Travel_____

Name (print)	Document type /Doc. name	Witness Name (print)	Date and Time Notarized _____ ___ _____ am / pm
Phone # / E-mail	Date of document	Witness Phone # / E-mail	Print of Right Thumb
Address	Satisfactory evidence of ID ☐ Driver's license ☐ Known Personally ☐ Credible Witness(es) ☐ Passport ☐ I.D. Card ☐ See Notes	Witness Address	
☐ ID. Issued by ☐ I.D. Number	☐ Expiration Date ☐ Issue Date	Notes	
Signer Signature		Witness Signature	

140
Service: ☐ Acknowledgment ☐ Oath/Affirmation ☐ Jurat ☐ Other/See Notes   Fee $_____ Travel_____

Name (print)	Document type /Doc. name	Witness Name (print)	Date and Time Notarized _____ ___ _____ am / pm
Phone # / E-mail	Date of document	Witness Phone # / E-mail	Print of Right Thumb
Address	Satisfactory evidence of ID ☐ Driver's license ☐ Known Personally ☐ Credible Witness(es) ☐ Passport ☐ I.D. Card ☐ See Notes	Witness Address	
☐ ID. Issued by ☐ I.D. Number	☐ Expiration Date ☐ Issue Date	Notes	
Signer Signature		Witness Signature	

NOTARY PUBLIC JOURNAL – LARGE ENTRIES | 73

141
Service: ☐ Acknowledgment ☐ Oath/Affirmation ☐ Jurat ☐ Other/See Notes Fee $_____ Travel_____

Name (print)	Document type /Doc. name	Witness Name (print)	Date and Time Notarized _____ ___ _____ am / pm
Phone # / E-mail	Date of document	Witness Phone # / E-mail	Print of Right Thumb
Address	Satisfactory evidence of ID ☐ Driver's license ☐ Known Personally ☐ Credible Witness(es) ☐ Passport ☐ I.D. Card ☐ See Notes	Witness Address	
☐ ID. Issued by ☐ I.D. Number	☐ Expiration Date ☐ Issue Date	Notes	
Signer Signature		Witness Signature	

142
Service: ☐ Acknowledgment ☐ Oath/Affirmation ☐ Jurat ☐ Other/See Notes Fee $_____ Travel_____

Name (print)	Document type /Doc. name	Witness Name (print)	Date and Time Notarized _____ ___ _____ am / pm
Phone # / E-mail	Date of document	Witness Phone # / E-mail	Print of Right Thumb
Address	Satisfactory evidence of ID ☐ Driver's license ☐ Known Personally ☐ Credible Witness(es) ☐ Passport ☐ I.D. Card ☐ See Notes	Witness Address	
☐ ID. Issued by ☐ I.D. Number	☐ Expiration Date ☐ Issue Date	Notes	
Signer Signature		Witness Signature	

74 | NOTARY PUBLIC JOURNAL – LARGE ENTRIES

143
Service: ☐ Acknowledgment ☐ Oath/Affirmation ☐ Jurat ☐ Other/See Notes Fee $_____ Travel_____

Name (print)	Document type /Doc. name	Witness Name (print)	Date and Time Notarized _____ ___ _____ am / pm
Phone # / E-mail	Date of document	Witness Phone # / E-mail	Print of Right Thumb
Address	Satisfactory evidence of ID ☐ Driver's license ☐ Known Personally ☐ Credible Witness(es) ☐ Passport ☐ I.D. Card ☐ See Notes	Witness Address	
☐ ID. Issued by ☐ I.D. Number	☐ Expiration Date ☐ Issue Date	Notes	
Signer Signature		Witness Signature	

144
Service: ☐ Acknowledgment ☐ Oath/Affirmation ☐ Jurat ☐ Other/See Notes Fee $_____ Travel_____

Name (print)	Document type /Doc. name	Witness Name (print)	Date and Time Notarized _____ ___ _____ am / pm
Phone # / E-mail	Date of document	Witness Phone # / E-mail	Print of Right Thumb
Address	Satisfactory evidence of ID ☐ Driver's license ☐ Known Personally ☐ Credible Witness(es) ☐ Passport ☐ I.D. Card ☐ See Notes	Witness Address	
☐ ID. Issued by ☐ I.D. Number	☐ Expiration Date ☐ Issue Date	Notes	
Signer Signature		Witness Signature	

NOTARY PUBLIC JOURNAL – LARGE ENTRIES | 75

145
Service: ☐ Acknowledgment ☐ Oath/Affirmation ☐ Jurat ☐ Other/See Notes Fee $_____ Travel_____

Name (print)	Document type /Doc. name	Witness Name (print)	Date and Time Notarized
			_____ ___ _____ am / pm
Phone # / E-mail	Date of document	Witness Phone # / E-mail	Print of Right Thumb
Address	Satisfactory evidence of ID ☐ Driver's license ☐ Known Personally ☐ Credible Witness(es) ☐ Passport ☐ I.D. Card ☐ See Notes	Witness Address	
☐ ID. Issued by ☐ I.D. Number	☐ Expiration Date ☐ Issue Date	Notes	
Signer Signature		Witness Signature	

146
Service: ☐ Acknowledgment ☐ Oath/Affirmation ☐ Jurat ☐ Other/See Notes Fee $_____ Travel_____

Name (print)	Document type /Doc. name	Witness Name (print)	Date and Time Notarized
			_____ ___ _____ am / pm
Phone # / E-mail	Date of document	Witness Phone # / E-mail	Print of Right Thumb
Address	Satisfactory evidence of ID ☐ Driver's license ☐ Known Personally ☐ Credible Witness(es) ☐ Passport ☐ I.D. Card ☐ See Notes	Witness Address	
☐ ID. Issued by ☐ I.D. Number	☐ Expiration Date ☐ Issue Date	Notes	
Signer Signature		Witness Signature	

NOTARY PUBLIC JOURNAL – LARGE ENTRIES

147

Service: ☐ Acknowledgment ☐ Oath/Affirmation ☐ Jurat ☐ Other/See Notes Fee $_____ Travel_____

Name (print)	Document type /Doc. name	Witness Name (print)	Date and Time Notarized _____ ___ _____ am / pm
Phone # / E-mail	Date of document	Witness Phone # / E-mail	Print of Right Thumb
Address	Satisfactory evidence of ID ☐ Driver's license ☐ Known Personally ☐ Credible Witness(es) ☐ Passport ☐ I.D. Card ☐ See Notes	Witness Address	
☐ ID. Issued by ☐ I.D. Number	☐ Expiration Date ☐ Issue Date	Notes	
Signer Signature		Witness Signature	

148

Service: ☐ Acknowledgment ☐ Oath/Affirmation ☐ Jurat ☐ Other/See Notes Fee $_____ Travel_____

Name (print)	Document type /Doc. name	Witness Name (print)	Date and Time Notarized _____ ___ _____ am / pm
Phone # / E-mail	Date of document	Witness Phone # / E-mail	Print of Right Thumb
Address	Satisfactory evidence of ID ☐ Driver's license ☐ Known Personally ☐ Credible Witness(es) ☐ Passport ☐ I.D. Card ☐ See Notes	Witness Address	
☐ ID. Issued by ☐ I.D. Number	☐ Expiration Date ☐ Issue Date	Notes	
Signer Signature		Witness Signature	

NOTARY PUBLIC JOURNAL – LARGE ENTRIES 77

149
Service: ☐ Acknowledgment ☐ Oath/Affirmation ☐ Jurat ☐ Other/See Notes Fee $_____ Travel_____

Name (print)	Document type /Doc. name	Witness Name (print)	Date and Time Notarized _____ ___ _____ am / pm
Phone # / E-mail	Date of document	Witness Phone # / E-mail	Print of Right Thumb
Address	Satisfactory evidence of ID ☐ Driver's license ☐ Known Personally ☐ Credible Witness(es) ☐ Passport ☐ I.D. Card ☐ See Notes	Witness Address	
☐ ID. Issued by ☐ I.D. Number	☐ Expiration Date ☐ Issue Date	Notes	
Signer Signature		Witness Signature	

150
Service: ☐ Acknowledgment ☐ Oath/Affirmation ☐ Jurat ☐ Other/See Notes Fee $_____ Travel_____

Name (print)	Document type /Doc. name	Witness Name (print)	Date and Time Notarized _____ ___ _____ am / pm
Phone # / E-mail	Date of document	Witness Phone # / E-mail	Print of Right Thumb
Address	Satisfactory evidence of ID ☐ Driver's license ☐ Known Personally ☐ Credible Witness(es) ☐ Passport ☐ I.D. Card ☐ See Notes	Witness Address	
☐ ID. Issued by ☐ I.D. Number	☐ Expiration Date ☐ Issue Date	Notes	
Signer Signature		Witness Signature	

NOTARY PUBLIC JOURNAL – LARGE ENTRIES

151
Service: ☐ Acknowledgment ☐ Oath/Affirmation ☐ Jurat ☐ Other/See Notes   Fee $_____   Travel_____

Name (print)	Document type /Doc. name	Witness Name (print)	Date and Time Notarized _____ ___ _____ am / pm
Phone # / E-mail	Date of document	Witness Phone # / E-mail	Print of Right Thumb
Address	Satisfactory evidence of ID ☐ Driver's license ☐ Known Personally ☐ Credible Witness(es) ☐ Passport ☐ I.D. Card ☐ See Notes	Witness Address	
☐ ID. Issued by ☐ I.D. Number	☐ Expiration Date ☐ Issue Date	Notes	
Signer Signature		Witness Signature	

152
Service: ☐ Acknowledgment ☐ Oath/Affirmation ☐ Jurat ☐ Other/See Notes   Fee $_____   Travel_____

Name (print)	Document type /Doc. name	Witness Name (print)	Date and Time Notarized _____ ___ _____ am / pm
Phone # / E-mail	Date of document	Witness Phone # / E-mail	Print of Right Thumb
Address	Satisfactory evidence of ID ☐ Driver's license ☐ Known Personally ☐ Credible Witness(es) ☐ Passport ☐ I.D. Card ☐ See Notes	Witness Address	
☐ ID. Issued by ☐ I.D. Number	☐ Expiration Date ☐ Issue Date	Notes	
Signer Signature		Witness Signature	

NOTARY PUBLIC JOURNAL – LARGE ENTRIES | 79

153
Service: ☐ Acknowledgment ☐ Oath/Affirmation ☐ Jurat ☐ Other/See Notes   Fee $_____   Travel_____

Name (print)	Document type /Doc. name	Witness Name (print)	Date and Time Notarized _____ ___ _____ am / pm
Phone # / E-mail	Date of document	Witness Phone # / E-mail	Print of Right Thumb
Address	Satisfactory evidence of ID ☐ Driver's license ☐ Known Personally ☐ Credible Witness(es) ☐ Passport ☐ I.D. Card ☐ See Notes	Witness Address	
☐ ID. Issued by ☐ I.D. Number	☐ Expiration Date ☐ Issue Date	Notes	
Signer Signature		Witness Signature	

154
Service: ☐ Acknowledgment ☐ Oath/Affirmation ☐ Jurat ☐ Other/See Notes   Fee $_____   Travel_____

Name (print)	Document type /Doc. name	Witness Name (print)	Date and Time Notarized _____ ___ _____ am / pm
Phone # / E-mail	Date of document	Witness Phone # / E-mail	Print of Right Thumb
Address	Satisfactory evidence of ID ☐ Driver's license ☐ Known Personally ☐ Credible Witness(es) ☐ Passport ☐ I.D. Card ☐ See Notes	Witness Address	
☐ ID. Issued by ☐ I.D. Number	☐ Expiration Date ☐ Issue Date	Notes	
Signer Signature		Witness Signature	

NOTARY PUBLIC JOURNAL – LARGE ENTRIES

155
Service: ☐ Acknowledgment   ☐ Oath/Affirmation   ☐ Jurat   ☐ Other/See Notes   Fee $_____   Travel_____

Name (print)	Document type /Doc. name	Witness Name (print)	Date and Time Notarized _____ ___ _____ am / pm
Phone # / E-mail	Date of document	Witness Phone # / E-mail	Print of Right Thumb
Address	Satisfactory evidence of ID ☐ Driver's license ☐ Known Personally ☐ Credible Witness(es) ☐ Passport ☐ I.D. Card ☐ See Notes	Witness Address	
☐ ID. Issued by ☐ I.D. Number	☐ Expiration Date ☐ Issue Date	Notes	
Signer Signature		Witness Signature	

156
Service: ☐ Acknowledgment   ☐ Oath/Affirmation   ☐ Jurat   ☐ Other/See Notes   Fee $_____   Travel_____

Name (print)	Document type /Doc. name	Witness Name (print)	Date and Time Notarized _____ ___ _____ am / pm
Phone # / E-mail	Date of document	Witness Phone # / E-mail	Print of Right Thumb
Address	Satisfactory evidence of ID ☐ Driver's license ☐ Known Personally ☐ Credible Witness(es) ☐ Passport ☐ I.D. Card ☐ See Notes	Witness Address	
☐ ID. Issued by ☐ I.D. Number	☐ Expiration Date ☐ Issue Date	Notes	
Signer Signature		Witness Signature	

NOTARY PUBLIC JOURNAL – LARGE ENTRIES

157
Service: ☐ Acknowledgment ☐ Oath/Affirmation ☐ Jurat ☐ Other/See Notes   Fee $_____   Travel_____

Name (print)	Document type /Doc. name	Witness Name (print)	Date and Time Notarized
			_____ ___ _____ am / pm
Phone # / E-mail	Date of document	Witness Phone # / E-mail	Print of Right Thumb
Address	Satisfactory evidence of ID ☐ Driver's license ☐ Known Personally ☐ Credible Witness(es) ☐ Passport ☐ I.D. Card ☐ See Notes	Witness Address	
☐ ID. Issued by ☐ I.D. Number	☐ Expiration Date ☐ Issue Date	Notes	
Signer Signature		Witness Signature	

158
Service: ☐ Acknowledgment ☐ Oath/Affirmation ☐ Jurat ☐ Other/See Notes   Fee $_____   Travel_____

Name (print)	Document type /Doc. name	Witness Name (print)	Date and Time Notarized
			_____ ___ _____ am / pm
Phone # / E-mail	Date of document	Witness Phone # / E-mail	Print of Right Thumb
Address	Satisfactory evidence of ID ☐ Driver's license ☐ Known Personally ☐ Credible Witness(es) ☐ Passport ☐ I.D. Card ☐ See Notes	Witness Address	
☐ ID. Issued by ☐ I.D. Number	☐ Expiration Date ☐ Issue Date	Notes	
Signer Signature		Witness Signature	

82 | NOTARY PUBLIC JOURNAL – LARGE ENTRIES

159

Service: ☐ Acknowledgment ☐ Oath/Affirmation ☐ Jurat ☐ Other/See Notes Fee $_____ Travel_____

Name (print)	Document type /Doc. name	Witness Name (print)	Date and Time Notarized _____ ___ _____ am / pm
Phone # / E-mail	Date of document	Witness Phone # / E-mail	Print of Right Thumb
Address	Satisfactory evidence of ID ☐ Driver's license ☐ Known Personally ☐ Credible Witness(es) ☐ Passport ☐ I.D. Card ☐ See Notes	Witness Address	
☐ ID. Issued by ☐ I.D. Number	☐ Expiration Date ☐ Issue Date	Notes	
Signer Signature		Witness Signature	

160

Service: ☐ Acknowledgment ☐ Oath/Affirmation ☐ Jurat ☐ Other/See Notes Fee $_____ Travel_____

Name (print)	Document type /Doc. name	Witness Name (print)	Date and Time Notarized _____ ___ _____ am / pm
Phone # / E-mail	Date of document	Witness Phone # / E-mail	Print of Right Thumb
Address	Satisfactory evidence of ID ☐ Driver's license ☐ Known Personally ☐ Credible Witness(es) ☐ Passport ☐ I.D. Card ☐ See Notes	Witness Address	
☐ ID. Issued by ☐ I.D. Number	☐ Expiration Date ☐ Issue Date	Notes	
Signer Signature		Witness Signature	

NOTARY PUBLIC JOURNAL – LARGE ENTRIES | 83

161

Service: ☐ Acknowledgment ☐ Oath/Affirmation ☐ Jurat ☐ Other/See Notes Fee $_____ Travel_____

Name (print)	Document type /Doc. name	Witness Name (print)	Date and Time Notarized _____ ___ _____ am / pm
Phone # / E-mail	Date of document	Witness Phone # / E-mail	Print of Right Thumb
Address	Satisfactory evidence of ID ☐ Driver's license ☐ Known Personally ☐ Credible Witness(es) ☐ Passport ☐ I.D. Card ☐ See Notes	Witness Address	
☐ ID. Issued by ☐ I.D. Number	☐ Expiration Date ☐ Issue Date	Notes	
Signer Signature		Witness Signature	

162

Service: ☐ Acknowledgment ☐ Oath/Affirmation ☐ Jurat ☐ Other/See Notes Fee $_____ Travel_____

Name (print)	Document type /Doc. name	Witness Name (print)	Date and Time Notarized _____ ___ _____ am / pm
Phone # / E-mail	Date of document	Witness Phone # / E-mail	Print of Right Thumb
Address	Satisfactory evidence of ID ☐ Driver's license ☐ Known Personally ☐ Credible Witness(es) ☐ Passport ☐ I.D. Card ☐ See Notes	Witness Address	
☐ ID. Issued by ☐ I.D. Number	☐ Expiration Date ☐ Issue Date	Notes	
Signer Signature		Witness Signature	

84 | NOTARY PUBLIC JOURNAL – LARGE ENTRIES

163

Service: ☐ Acknowledgment ☐ Oath/Affirmation ☐ Jurat ☐ Other/See Notes   Fee $_____   Travel_____

Name (print)	Document type /Doc. name	Witness Name (print)	Date and Time Notarized _____ ___ _____ am / pm
Phone # / E-mail	Date of document	Witness Phone # / E-mail	Print of Right Thumb
Address	Satisfactory evidence of ID ☐ Driver's license ☐ Known Personally ☐ Credible Witness(es) ☐ Passport ☐ I.D. Card ☐ See Notes	Witness Address	
☐ ID. Issued by ☐ I.D. Number	☐ Expiration Date ☐ Issue Date	Notes	
Signer Signature		Witness Signature	

164

Service: ☐ Acknowledgment ☐ Oath/Affirmation ☐ Jurat ☐ Other/See Notes   Fee $_____   Travel_____

Name (print)	Document type /Doc. name	Witness Name (print)	Date and Time Notarized _____ ___ _____ am / pm
Phone # / E-mail	Date of document	Witness Phone # / E-mail	Print of Right Thumb
Address	Satisfactory evidence of ID ☐ Driver's license ☐ Known Personally ☐ Credible Witness(es) ☐ Passport ☐ I.D. Card ☐ See Notes	Witness Address	
☐ ID. Issued by ☐ I.D. Number	☐ Expiration Date ☐ Issue Date	Notes	
Signer Signature		Witness Signature	

NOTARY PUBLIC JOURNAL – LARGE ENTRIES | 85

165

Service: ☐ Acknowledgment ☐ Oath/Affirmation ☐ Jurat ☐ Other/See Notes Fee $_____ Travel_____

Name (print)	Document type /Doc. name	Witness Name (print)	Date and Time Notarized _____ ___ _____ am / pm
Phone # / E-mail	Date of document	Witness Phone # / E-mail	Print of Right Thumb
Address	Satisfactory evidence of ID ☐ Driver's license ☐ Known Personally ☐ Credible Witness(es) ☐ Passport ☐ I.D. Card ☐ See Notes	Witness Address	
☐ ID. Issued by ☐ I.D. Number	☐ Expiration Date ☐ Issue Date	Notes	
Signer Signature		Witness Signature	

166

Service: ☐ Acknowledgment ☐ Oath/Affirmation ☐ Jurat ☐ Other/See Notes Fee $_____ Travel_____

Name (print)	Document type /Doc. name	Witness Name (print)	Date and Time Notarized _____ ___ _____ am / pm
Phone # / E-mail	Date of document	Witness Phone # / E-mail	Print of Right Thumb
Address	Satisfactory evidence of ID ☐ Driver's license ☐ Known Personally ☐ Credible Witness(es) ☐ Passport ☐ I.D. Card ☐ See Notes	Witness Address	
☐ ID. Issued by ☐ I.D. Number	☐ Expiration Date ☐ Issue Date	Notes	
Signer Signature		Witness Signature	

NOTARY PUBLIC JOURNAL – LARGE ENTRIES

167

Service: ☐ Acknowledgment ☐ Oath/Affirmation ☐ Jurat ☐ Other/See Notes   Fee $_____   Travel_____

Name (print)	Document type /Doc. name	Witness Name (print)	Date and Time Notarized _____ ___ _____ am / pm
Phone # / E-mail	Date of document	Witness Phone # / E-mail	Print of Right Thumb
Address	Satisfactory evidence of ID ☐ Driver's license ☐ Known Personally ☐ Credible Witness(es) ☐ Passport ☐ I.D. Card ☐ See Notes	Witness Address	
☐ ID. Issued by ☐ I.D. Number	☐ Expiration Date ☐ Issue Date	Notes	
Signer Signature		Witness Signature	

168

Service: ☐ Acknowledgment ☐ Oath/Affirmation ☐ Jurat ☐ Other/See Notes   Fee $_____   Travel_____

Name (print)	Document type /Doc. name	Witness Name (print)	Date and Time Notarized _____ ___ _____ am / pm
Phone # / E-mail	Date of document	Witness Phone # / E-mail	Print of Right Thumb
Address	Satisfactory evidence of ID ☐ Driver's license ☐ Known Personally ☐ Credible Witness(es) ☐ Passport ☐ I.D. Card ☐ See Notes	Witness Address	
☐ ID. Issued by ☐ I.D. Number	☐ Expiration Date ☐ Issue Date	Notes	
Signer Signature		Witness Signature	

NOTARY PUBLIC JOURNAL – LARGE ENTRIES | 87

169
Service: ☐ Acknowledgment ☐ Oath/Affirmation ☐ Jurat ☐ Other/See Notes Fee $_____ Travel_____

Name (print)	Document type /Doc. name	Witness Name (print)	Date and Time Notarized _____ ___ _____ am / pm
Phone # / E-mail	Date of document	Witness Phone # / E-mail	Print of Right Thumb
Address	Satisfactory evidence of ID ☐ Driver's license ☐ Known Personally ☐ Credible Witness(es) ☐ Passport ☐ I.D. Card ☐ See Notes	Witness Address	
☐ ID. Issued by ☐ I.D. Number	☐ Expiration Date ☐ Issue Date	Notes	
Signer Signature		Witness Signature	

170
Service: ☐ Acknowledgment ☐ Oath/Affirmation ☐ Jurat ☐ Other/See Notes Fee $_____ Travel_____

Name (print)	Document type /Doc. name	Witness Name (print)	Date and Time Notarized _____ ___ _____ am / pm
Phone # / E-mail	Date of document	Witness Phone # / E-mail	Print of Right Thumb
Address	Satisfactory evidence of ID ☐ Driver's license ☐ Known Personally ☐ Credible Witness(es) ☐ Passport ☐ I.D. Card ☐ See Notes	Witness Address	
☐ ID. Issued by ☐ I.D. Number	☐ Expiration Date ☐ Issue Date	Notes	
Signer Signature		Witness Signature	

NOTARY PUBLIC JOURNAL – LARGE ENTRIES

171

Service: ☐ Acknowledgment ☐ Oath/Affirmation ☐ Jurat ☐ Other/See Notes   Fee $_____   Travel_____

Name (print)	Document type /Doc. name	Witness Name (print)	Date and Time Notarized _____ ___ _____ am / pm
Phone # / E-mail	Date of document	Witness Phone # / E-mail	Print of Right Thumb
Address	Satisfactory evidence of ID ☐ Driver's license ☐ Known Personally ☐ Credible Witness(es) ☐ Passport ☐ I.D. Card ☐ See Notes	Witness Address	
☐ ID. Issued by ☐ I.D. Number	☐ Expiration Date ☐ Issue Date	Notes	
Signer Signature		Witness Signature	

172

Service: ☐ Acknowledgment ☐ Oath/Affirmation ☐ Jurat ☐ Other/See Notes   Fee $_____   Travel_____

Name (print)	Document type /Doc. name	Witness Name (print)	Date and Time Notarized _____ ___ _____ am / pm
Phone # / E-mail	Date of document	Witness Phone # / E-mail	Print of Right Thumb
Address	Satisfactory evidence of ID ☐ Driver's license ☐ Known Personally ☐ Credible Witness(es) ☐ Passport ☐ I.D. Card ☐ See Notes	Witness Address	
☐ ID. Issued by ☐ I.D. Number	☐ Expiration Date ☐ Issue Date	Notes	
Signer Signature		Witness Signature	

NOTARY PUBLIC JOURNAL – LARGE ENTRIES | 89

173
Service: ☐ Acknowledgment ☐ Oath/Affirmation ☐ Jurat ☐ Other/See Notes   Fee $_____ Travel_____

Name (print)	Document type /Doc. name	Witness Name (print)	Date and Time Notarized _____ ___ _____ am / pm
Phone # / E-mail	Date of document	Witness Phone # / E-mail	Print of Right Thumb
Address	Satisfactory evidence of ID ☐ Driver's license ☐ Known Personally ☐ Credible Witness(es) ☐ Passport ☐ I.D. Card ☐ See Notes	Witness Address	
☐ ID. Issued by ☐ I.D. Number	☐ Expiration Date ☐ Issue Date	Notes	
Signer Signature		Witness Signature	

174
Service: ☐ Acknowledgment ☐ Oath/Affirmation ☐ Jurat ☐ Other/See Notes   Fee $_____ Travel_____

Name (print)	Document type /Doc. name	Witness Name (print)	Date and Time Notarized _____ ___ _____ am / pm
Phone # / E-mail	Date of document	Witness Phone # / E-mail	Print of Right Thumb
Address	Satisfactory evidence of ID ☐ Driver's license ☐ Known Personally ☐ Credible Witness(es) ☐ Passport ☐ I.D. Card ☐ See Notes	Witness Address	
☐ ID. Issued by ☐ I.D. Number	☐ Expiration Date ☐ Issue Date	Notes	
Signer Signature		Witness Signature	

NOTARY PUBLIC JOURNAL – LARGE ENTRIES

175
Service: ☐ Acknowledgment ☐ Oath/Affirmation ☐ Jurat ☐ Other/See Notes   Fee $_____   Travel _____

Name (print)	Document type /Doc. name	Witness Name (print)	Date and Time Notarized _____ ___ _____ am / pm
Phone # / E-mail	Date of document	Witness Phone # / E-mail	Print of Right Thumb
Address	Satisfactory evidence of ID ☐ Driver's license ☐ Known Personally ☐ Credible Witness(es) ☐ Passport ☐ I.D. Card ☐ See Notes	Witness Address	
☐ ID. Issued by ☐ I.D. Number	☐ Expiration Date ☐ Issue Date	Notes	
Signer Signature		Witness Signature	

176
Service: ☐ Acknowledgment ☐ Oath/Affirmation ☐ Jurat ☐ Other/See Notes   Fee $_____   Travel _____

Name (print)	Document type /Doc. name	Witness Name (print)	Date and Time Notarized _____ ___ _____ am / pm
Phone # / E-mail	Date of document	Witness Phone # / E-mail	Print of Right Thumb
Address	Satisfactory evidence of ID ☐ Driver's license ☐ Known Personally ☐ Credible Witness(es) ☐ Passport ☐ I.D. Card ☐ See Notes	Witness Address	
☐ ID. Issued by ☐ I.D. Number	☐ Expiration Date ☐ Issue Date	Notes	
Signer Signature		Witness Signature	

NOTARY PUBLIC JOURNAL – LARGE ENTRIES

177
Service: ☐ Acknowledgment ☐ Oath/Affirmation ☐ Jurat ☐ Other/See Notes   Fee $_____   Travel_____

Name (print)	Document type /Doc. name	Witness Name (print)	Date and Time Notarized
			_____ ___ _____ am / pm
Phone # / E-mail	Date of document	Witness Phone # / E-mail	Print of Right Thumb
Address	Satisfactory evidence of ID ☐ Driver's license ☐ Known Personally ☐ Credible Witness(es) ☐ Passport ☐ I.D. Card ☐ See Notes	Witness Address	
☐ ID. Issued by ☐ I.D. Number	☐ Expiration Date ☐ Issue Date	Notes	
Signer Signature		Witness Signature	

178
Service: ☐ Acknowledgment ☐ Oath/Affirmation ☐ Jurat ☐ Other/See Notes   Fee $_____   Travel_____

Name (print)	Document type /Doc. name	Witness Name (print)	Date and Time Notarized
			_____ ___ _____ am / pm
Phone # / E-mail	Date of document	Witness Phone # / E-mail	Print of Right Thumb
Address	Satisfactory evidence of ID ☐ Driver's license ☐ Known Personally ☐ Credible Witness(es) ☐ Passport ☐ I.D. Card ☐ See Notes	Witness Address	
☐ ID. Issued by ☐ I.D. Number	☐ Expiration Date ☐ Issue Date	Notes	
Signer Signature		Witness Signature	

NOTARY PUBLIC JOURNAL – LARGE ENTRIES

179

Service: ☐ Acknowledgment   ☐ Oath/Affirmation   ☐ Jurat   ☐ Other/See Notes   Fee $_____   Travel_____

Name (print)	Document type /Doc. name	Witness Name (print)	Date and Time Notarized _____ ___ _____ am / pm
Phone # / E-mail	Date of document	Witness Phone # / E-mail	Print of Right Thumb
Address	Satisfactory evidence of ID ☐ Driver's license ☐ Known Personally ☐ Credible Witness(es) ☐ Passport ☐ I.D. Card ☐ See Notes	Witness Address	
☐ ID. Issued by ☐ I.D. Number	☐ Expiration Date ☐ Issue Date	Notes	
Signer Signature		Witness Signature	

180

Service: ☐ Acknowledgment   ☐ Oath/Affirmation   ☐ Jurat   ☐ Other/See Notes   Fee $_____   Travel_____

Name (print)	Document type /Doc. name	Witness Name (print)	Date and Time Notarized _____ ___ _____ am / pm
Phone # / E-mail	Date of document	Witness Phone # / E-mail	Print of Right Thumb
Address	Satisfactory evidence of ID ☐ Driver's license ☐ Known Personally ☐ Credible Witness(es) ☐ Passport ☐ I.D. Card ☐ See Notes	Witness Address	
☐ ID. Issued by ☐ I.D. Number	☐ Expiration Date ☐ Issue Date	Notes	
Signer Signature		Witness Signature	

NOTARY PUBLIC JOURNAL – LARGE ENTRIES

181
Service: ☐ Acknowledgment ☐ Oath/Affirmation ☐ Jurat ☐ Other/See Notes   Fee $_____   Travel_____

Name (print)	Document type /Doc. name	Witness Name (print)	Date and Time Notarized _____ ___ _____ am / pm
Phone # / E-mail	Date of document	Witness Phone # / E-mail	Print of Right Thumb
Address	Satisfactory evidence of ID ☐ Driver's license ☐ Known Personally ☐ Credible Witness(es) ☐ Passport ☐ I.D. Card ☐ See Notes	Witness Address	
☐ ID. Issued by ☐ I.D. Number	☐ Expiration Date ☐ Issue Date	Notes	
Signer Signature		Witness Signature	

182
Service: ☐ Acknowledgment ☐ Oath/Affirmation ☐ Jurat ☐ Other/See Notes   Fee $_____   Travel_____

Name (print)	Document type /Doc. name	Witness Name (print)	Date and Time Notarized _____ ___ _____ am / pm
Phone # / E-mail	Date of document	Witness Phone # / E-mail	Print of Right Thumb
Address	Satisfactory evidence of ID ☐ Driver's license ☐ Known Personally ☐ Credible Witness(es) ☐ Passport ☐ I.D. Card ☐ See Notes	Witness Address	
☐ ID. Issued by ☐ I.D. Number	☐ Expiration Date ☐ Issue Date	Notes	
Signer Signature		Witness Signature	

NOTARY PUBLIC JOURNAL – LARGE ENTRIES

183

Service: ☐ **Acknowledgment** ☐ **Oath/Affirmation** ☐ **Jurat** ☐ **Other/See Notes** **Fee $**_____ **Travel**_____

Name (print)	Document type /Doc. name	Witness Name (print)	Date and Time Notarized _____ ___ _____ am / pm
Phone # / E-mail	Date of document	Witness Phone # / E-mail	Print of Right Thumb
Address	Satisfactory evidence of ID ☐ Driver's license ☐ Known Personally ☐ Credible Witness(es) ☐ Passport ☐ I.D. Card ☐ See Notes	Witness Address	
☐ ID. Issued by ☐ I.D. Number	☐ Expiration Date ☐ Issue Date	Notes	
Signer Signature		Witness Signature	

184

Service: ☐ **Acknowledgment** ☐ **Oath/Affirmation** ☐ **Jurat** ☐ **Other/See Notes** **Fee $**_____ **Travel**_____

Name (print)	Document type /Doc. name	Witness Name (print)	Date and Time Notarized _____ ___ _____ am / pm
Phone # / E-mail	Date of document	Witness Phone # / E-mail	Print of Right Thumb
Address	Satisfactory evidence of ID ☐ Driver's license ☐ Known Personally ☐ Credible Witness(es) ☐ Passport ☐ I.D. Card ☐ See Notes	Witness Address	
☐ ID. Issued by ☐ I.D. Number	☐ Expiration Date ☐ Issue Date	Notes	
Signer Signature		Witness Signature	

NOTARY PUBLIC JOURNAL – LARGE ENTRIES 95

185
Service: ☐ Acknowledgment ☐ Oath/Affirmation ☐ Jurat ☐ Other/See Notes   Fee $_____   Travel_____

Name (print)	Document type /Doc. name	Witness Name (print)	Date and Time Notarized _____ ___ _____ am / pm
Phone # / E-mail	Date of document	Witness Phone # / E-mail	Print of Right Thumb
Address	Satisfactory evidence of ID ☐ Driver's license ☐ Known Personally ☐ Credible Witness(es) ☐ Passport ☐ I.D. Card ☐ See Notes	Witness Address	
☐ ID. Issued by ☐ I.D. Number	☐ Expiration Date ☐ Issue Date	Notes	
Signer Signature		Witness Signature	

186
Service: ☐ Acknowledgment ☐ Oath/Affirmation ☐ Jurat ☐ Other/See Notes   Fee $_____   Travel_____

Name (print)	Document type /Doc. name	Witness Name (print)	Date and Time Notarized _____ ___ _____ am / pm
Phone # / E-mail	Date of document	Witness Phone # / E-mail	Print of Right Thumb
Address	Satisfactory evidence of ID ☐ Driver's license ☐ Known Personally ☐ Credible Witness(es) ☐ Passport ☐ I.D. Card ☐ See Notes	Witness Address	
☐ ID. Issued by ☐ I.D. Number	☐ Expiration Date ☐ Issue Date	Notes	
Signer Signature		Witness Signature	

NOTARY PUBLIC JOURNAL – LARGE ENTRIES

187

Service: ☐ Acknowledgment ☐ Oath/Affirmation ☐ Jurat ☐ Other/See Notes Fee $_____ Travel_____

Name (print)	Document type /Doc. name	Witness Name (print)	Date and Time Notarized _____ ___ _____ am / pm
Phone # / E-mail	Date of document	Witness Phone # / E-mail	Print of Right Thumb
Address	Satisfactory evidence of ID ☐ Driver's license ☐ Known Personally ☐ Credible Witness(es) ☐ Passport ☐ I.D. Card ☐ See Notes	Witness Address	
☐ ID. Issued by ☐ I.D. Number	☐ Expiration Date ☐ Issue Date	Notes	
Signer Signature		Witness Signature	

188

Service: ☐ Acknowledgment ☐ Oath/Affirmation ☐ Jurat ☐ Other/See Notes Fee $_____ Travel_____

Name (print)	Document type /Doc. name	Witness Name (print)	Date and Time Notarized _____ ___ _____ am / pm
Phone # / E-mail	Date of document	Witness Phone # / E-mail	Print of Right Thumb
Address	Satisfactory evidence of ID ☐ Driver's license ☐ Known Personally ☐ Credible Witness(es) ☐ Passport ☐ I.D. Card ☐ See Notes	Witness Address	
☐ ID. Issued by ☐ I.D. Number	☐ Expiration Date ☐ Issue Date	Notes	
Signer Signature		Witness Signature	

NOTARY PUBLIC JOURNAL – LARGE ENTRIES | 97

189
Service: ☐ Acknowledgment ☐ Oath/Affirmation ☐ Jurat ☐ Other/See Notes Fee $_____ Travel_____

Name (print)	Document type /Doc. name	Witness Name (print)	Date and Time Notarized _____ ___ _____ am / pm
Phone # / E-mail	Date of document	Witness Phone # / E-mail	Print of Right Thumb
Address	Satisfactory evidence of ID ☐ Driver's license ☐ Known Personally ☐ Credible Witness(es) ☐ Passport ☐ I.D. Card ☐ See Notes	Witness Address	
☐ ID. Issued by ☐ I.D. Number	☐ Expiration Date ☐ Issue Date	Notes	
Signer Signature		Witness Signature	

190
Service: ☐ Acknowledgment ☐ Oath/Affirmation ☐ Jurat ☐ Other/See Notes Fee $_____ Travel_____

Name (print)	Document type /Doc. name	Witness Name (print)	Date and Time Notarized _____ ___ _____ am / pm
Phone # / E-mail	Date of document	Witness Phone # / E-mail	Print of Right Thumb
Address	Satisfactory evidence of ID ☐ Driver's license ☐ Known Personally ☐ Credible Witness(es) ☐ Passport ☐ I.D. Card ☐ See Notes	Witness Address	
☐ ID. Issued by ☐ I.D. Number	☐ Expiration Date ☐ Issue Date	Notes	
Signer Signature		Witness Signature	

NOTARY PUBLIC JOURNAL – LARGE ENTRIES

191

Service: ☐ Acknowledgment ☐ Oath/Affirmation ☐ Jurat ☐ Other/See Notes   Fee $_____   Travel_____

Name (print)	Document type /Doc. name	Witness Name (print)	Date and Time Notarized _____ ___ _____ am / pm
Phone # / E-mail	Date of document	Witness Phone # / E-mail	Print of Right Thumb
Address	Satisfactory evidence of ID ☐ Driver's license ☐ Known Personally ☐ Credible Witness(es) ☐ Passport ☐ I.D. Card ☐ See Notes	Witness Address	
☐ ID. Issued by ☐ I.D. Number	☐ Expiration Date ☐ Issue Date	Notes	
Signer Signature		Witness Signature	

192

Service: ☐ Acknowledgment ☐ Oath/Affirmation ☐ Jurat ☐ Other/See Notes   Fee $_____   Travel_____

Name (print)	Document type /Doc. name	Witness Name (print)	Date and Time Notarized _____ ___ _____ am / pm
Phone # / E-mail	Date of document	Witness Phone # / E-mail	Print of Right Thumb
Address	Satisfactory evidence of ID ☐ Driver's license ☐ Known Personally ☐ Credible Witness(es) ☐ Passport ☐ I.D. Card ☐ See Notes	Witness Address	
☐ ID. Issued by ☐ I.D. Number	☐ Expiration Date ☐ Issue Date	Notes	
Signer Signature		Witness Signature	

NOTARY PUBLIC JOURNAL – LARGE ENTRIES

193

Service: ☐ Acknowledgment ☐ Oath/Affirmation ☐ Jurat ☐ Other/See Notes Fee $_____ Travel_____

Name (print)	Document type /Doc. name	Witness Name (print)	Date and Time Notarized _____ ___ _____ am / pm
Phone # / E-mail	Date of document	Witness Phone # / E-mail	Print of Right Thumb
Address	Satisfactory evidence of ID ☐ Driver's license ☐ Known Personally ☐ Credible Witness(es) ☐ Passport ☐ I.D. Card ☐ See Notes	Witness Address	
☐ ID. Issued by ☐ I.D. Number	☐ Expiration Date ☐ Issue Date	Notes	
Signer Signature		Witness Signature	

194

Service: ☐ Acknowledgment ☐ Oath/Affirmation ☐ Jurat ☐ Other/See Notes Fee $_____ Travel_____

Name (print)	Document type /Doc. name	Witness Name (print)	Date and Time Notarized _____ ___ _____ am / pm
Phone # / E-mail	Date of document	Witness Phone # / E-mail	Print of Right Thumb
Address	Satisfactory evidence of ID ☐ Driver's license ☐ Known Personally ☐ Credible Witness(es) ☐ Passport ☐ I.D. Card ☐ See Notes	Witness Address	
☐ ID. Issued by ☐ I.D. Number	☐ Expiration Date ☐ Issue Date	Notes	
Signer Signature		Witness Signature	

NOTARY PUBLIC JOURNAL – LARGE ENTRIES

195

Service: ☐ Acknowledgment ☐ Oath/Affirmation ☐ Jurat ☐ Other/See Notes   Fee $_____   Travel_____

Name (print)	Document type /Doc. name	Witness Name (print)	Date and Time Notarized _____ ___ _____ am / pm
Phone # / E-mail	Date of document	Witness Phone # / E-mail	Print of Right Thumb
Address	Satisfactory evidence of ID ☐ Driver's license ☐ Known Personally ☐ Credible Witness(es) ☐ Passport ☐ I.D. Card ☐ See Notes	Witness Address	
☐ ID. Issued by ☐ I.D. Number	☐ Expiration Date ☐ Issue Date	Notes	
Signer Signature		Witness Signature	

196

Service: ☐ Acknowledgment ☐ Oath/Affirmation ☐ Jurat ☐ Other/See Notes   Fee $_____   Travel_____

Name (print)	Document type /Doc. name	Witness Name (print)	Date and Time Notarized _____ ___ _____ am / pm
Phone # / E-mail	Date of document	Witness Phone # / E-mail	Print of Right Thumb
Address	Satisfactory evidence of ID ☐ Driver's license ☐ Known Personally ☐ Credible Witness(es) ☐ Passport ☐ I.D. Card ☐ See Notes	Witness Address	
☐ ID. Issued by ☐ I.D. Number	☐ Expiration Date ☐ Issue Date	Notes	
Signer Signature		Witness Signature	

NOTARY PUBLIC JOURNAL – LARGE ENTRIES | 101

197

Service: ☐ Acknowledgment ☐ Oath/Affirmation ☐ Jurat ☐ Other/See Notes Fee $_____ Travel_____

Name (print)	Document type /Doc. name	Witness Name (print)	Date and Time Notarized _____ ___ _____ am / pm
Phone # / E-mail	Date of document	Witness Phone # / E-mail	Print of Right Thumb
Address	Satisfactory evidence of ID ☐ Driver's license ☐ Known Personally ☐ Credible Witness(es) ☐ Passport ☐ I.D. Card ☐ See Notes	Witness Address	
☐ ID. Issued by ☐ I.D. Number	☐ Expiration Date ☐ Issue Date	Notes	
Signer Signature		Witness Signature	

198

Service: ☐ Acknowledgment ☐ Oath/Affirmation ☐ Jurat ☐ Other/See Notes Fee $_____ Travel_____

Name (print)	Document type /Doc. name	Witness Name (print)	Date and Time Notarized _____ ___ _____ am / pm
Phone # / E-mail	Date of document	Witness Phone # / E-mail	Print of Right Thumb
Address	Satisfactory evidence of ID ☐ Driver's license ☐ Known Personally ☐ Credible Witness(es) ☐ Passport ☐ I.D. Card ☐ See Notes	Witness Address	
☐ ID. Issued by ☐ I.D. Number	☐ Expiration Date ☐ Issue Date	Notes	
Signer Signature		Witness Signature	

NOTARY PUBLIC JOURNAL – LARGE ENTRIES

199

Service: ☐ Acknowledgment ☐ Oath/Affirmation ☐ Jurat ☐ Other/See Notes   Fee $_____   Travel_____

Name (print)	Document type /Doc. name	Witness Name (print)	Date and Time Notarized _____ ___ _____ am / pm
Phone # / E-mail	Date of document	Witness Phone # / E-mail	Print of Right Thumb
Address	Satisfactory evidence of ID ☐ Driver's license ☐ Known Personally ☐ Credible Witness(es) ☐ Passport ☐ I.D. Card ☐ See Notes	Witness Address	
☐ ID. Issued by ☐ I.D. Number	☐ Expiration Date ☐ Issue Date	Notes	
Signer Signature		Witness Signature	

200

Service: ☐ Acknowledgment ☐ Oath/Affirmation ☐ Jurat ☐ Other/See Notes   Fee $_____   Travel_____

Name (print)	Document type /Doc. name	Witness Name (print)	Date and Time Notarized _____ ___ _____ am / pm
Phone # / E-mail	Date of document	Witness Phone # / E-mail	Print of Right Thumb
Address	Satisfactory evidence of ID ☐ Driver's license ☐ Known Personally ☐ Credible Witness(es) ☐ Passport ☐ I.D. Card ☐ See Notes	Witness Address	
☐ ID. Issued by ☐ I.D. Number	☐ Expiration Date ☐ Issue Date	Notes	
Signer Signature		Witness Signature	

NOTARY PUBLIC JOURNAL – LARGE ENTRIES

201
Service: ☐ Acknowledgment ☐ Oath/Affirmation ☐ Jurat ☐ Other/See Notes Fee $_____ Travel_____

Name (print)	Document type /Doc. name	Witness Name (print)	Date and Time Notarized _____ ___ _____ am / pm
Phone # / E-mail	Date of document	Witness Phone # / E-mail	Print of Right Thumb
Address	Satisfactory evidence of ID ☐ Driver's license ☐ Known Personally ☐ Credible Witness(es) ☐ Passport ☐ I.D. Card ☐ See Notes	Witness Address	
☐ ID. Issued by ☐ I.D. Number	☐ Expiration Date ☐ Issue Date	Notes	
Signer Signature		Witness Signature	

202
Service: ☐ Acknowledgment ☐ Oath/Affirmation ☐ Jurat ☐ Other/See Notes Fee $_____ Travel_____

Name (print)	Document type /Doc. name	Witness Name (print)	Date and Time Notarized _____ ___ _____ am / pm
Phone # / E-mail	Date of document	Witness Phone # / E-mail	Print of Right Thumb
Address	Satisfactory evidence of ID ☐ Driver's license ☐ Known Personally ☐ Credible Witness(es) ☐ Passport ☐ I.D. Card ☐ See Notes	Witness Address	
☐ ID. Issued by ☐ I.D. Number	☐ Expiration Date ☐ Issue Date	Notes	
Signer Signature		Witness Signature	

NOTARY PUBLIC JOURNAL – LARGE ENTRIES

203

Service: ☐ Acknowledgment ☐ Oath/Affirmation ☐ Jurat ☐ Other/See Notes Fee $ _____ Travel _____

Name (print)	Document type /Doc. name	Witness Name (print)	Date and Time Notarized _____ ___ _____ am / pm
Phone # / E-mail	Date of document	Witness Phone # / E-mail	Print of Right Thumb
Address	Satisfactory evidence of ID ☐ Driver's license ☐ Known Personally ☐ Credible Witness(es) ☐ Passport ☐ I.D. Card ☐ See Notes	Witness Address	
☐ ID. Issued by ☐ I.D. Number	☐ Expiration Date ☐ Issue Date	Notes	
Signer Signature		Witness Signature	

204

Service: ☐ Acknowledgment ☐ Oath/Affirmation ☐ Jurat ☐ Other/See Notes Fee $ _____ Travel _____

Name (print)	Document type /Doc. name	Witness Name (print)	Date and Time Notarized _____ ___ _____ am / pm
Phone # / E-mail	Date of document	Witness Phone # / E-mail	Print of Right Thumb
Address	Satisfactory evidence of ID ☐ Driver's license ☐ Known Personally ☐ Credible Witness(es) ☐ Passport ☐ I.D. Card ☐ See Notes	Witness Address	
☐ ID. Issued by ☐ I.D. Number	☐ Expiration Date ☐ Issue Date	Notes	
Signer Signature		Witness Signature	

NOTARY PUBLIC JOURNAL – LARGE ENTRIES | 105

205 — Service: ☐ Acknowledgment ☐ Oath/Affirmation ☐ Jurat ☐ Other/See Notes Fee $_____ Travel_____

Name (print)	Document type /Doc. name	Witness Name (print)	Date and Time Notarized _____ ___ _____ am / pm
Phone # / E-mail	Date of document	Witness Phone # / E-mail	Print of Right Thumb
Address	Satisfactory evidence of ID ☐ Driver's license ☐ Known Personally ☐ Credible Witness(es) ☐ Passport ☐ I.D. Card ☐ See Notes	Witness Address	
☐ ID. Issued by ☐ I.D. Number	☐ Expiration Date ☐ Issue Date	Notes	
Signer Signature		Witness Signature	

206 — Service: ☐ Acknowledgment ☐ Oath/Affirmation ☐ Jurat ☐ Other/See Notes Fee $_____ Travel_____

Name (print)	Document type /Doc. name	Witness Name (print)	Date and Time Notarized _____ ___ _____ am / pm
Phone # / E-mail	Date of document	Witness Phone # / E-mail	Print of Right Thumb
Address	Satisfactory evidence of ID ☐ Driver's license ☐ Known Personally ☐ Credible Witness(es) ☐ Passport ☐ I.D. Card ☐ See Notes	Witness Address	
☐ ID. Issued by ☐ I.D. Number	☐ Expiration Date ☐ Issue Date	Notes	
Signer Signature		Witness Signature	

NOTARY PUBLIC JOURNAL – LARGE ENTRIES

207

Service: ☐ Acknowledgment ☐ Oath/Affirmation ☐ Jurat ☐ Other/See Notes Fee $_____ Travel_____

Name (print)	Document type /Doc. name	Witness Name (print)	Date and Time Notarized _____ ___ _____ am / pm
Phone # / E-mail	Date of document	Witness Phone # / E-mail	Print of Right Thumb
Address	Satisfactory evidence of ID ☐ Driver's license ☐ Known Personally ☐ Credible Witness(es) ☐ Passport ☐ I.D. Card ☐ See Notes	Witness Address	
☐ ID. Issued by ☐ I.D. Number	☐ Expiration Date ☐ Issue Date	Notes	
Signer Signature		Witness Signature	

208

Service: ☐ Acknowledgment ☐ Oath/Affirmation ☐ Jurat ☐ Other/See Notes Fee $_____ Travel_____

Name (print)	Document type /Doc. name	Witness Name (print)	Date and Time Notarized _____ ___ _____ am / pm
Phone # / E-mail	Date of document	Witness Phone # / E-mail	Print of Right Thumb
Address	Satisfactory evidence of ID ☐ Driver's license ☐ Known Personally ☐ Credible Witness(es) ☐ Passport ☐ I.D. Card ☐ See Notes	Witness Address	
☐ ID. Issued by ☐ I.D. Number	☐ Expiration Date ☐ Issue Date	Notes	
Signer Signature		Witness Signature	

NOTARY PUBLIC JOURNAL – LARGE ENTRIES

209
Service: ☐ Acknowledgment ☐ Oath/Affirmation ☐ Jurat ☐ Other/See Notes   Fee $_____ Travel_____

Name (print)	Document type /Doc. name	Witness Name (print)	Date and Time Notarized _____ ___ _____ am / pm
Phone # / E-mail	Date of document	Witness Phone # / E-mail	Print of Right Thumb
Address	Satisfactory evidence of ID ☐ Driver's license ☐ Known Personally ☐ Credible Witness(es) ☐ Passport ☐ I.D. Card ☐ See Notes	Witness Address	
☐ ID. Issued by ☐ I.D. Number	☐ Expiration Date ☐ Issue Date	Notes	
Signer Signature		Witness Signature	

210
Service: ☐ Acknowledgment ☐ Oath/Affirmation ☐ Jurat ☐ Other/See Notes   Fee $_____ Travel_____

Name (print)	Document type /Doc. name	Witness Name (print)	Date and Time Notarized _____ ___ _____ am / pm
Phone # / E-mail	Date of document	Witness Phone # / E-mail	Print of Right Thumb
Address	Satisfactory evidence of ID ☐ Driver's license ☐ Known Personally ☐ Credible Witness(es) ☐ Passport ☐ I.D. Card ☐ See Notes	Witness Address	
☐ ID. Issued by ☐ I.D. Number	☐ Expiration Date ☐ Issue Date	Notes	
Signer Signature		Witness Signature	

NOTARY PUBLIC JOURNAL – LARGE ENTRIES

211

Service: ☐ Acknowledgment ☐ Oath/Affirmation ☐ Jurat ☐ Other/See Notes Fee $_____ Travel_____

Name (print)	Document type /Doc. name	Witness Name (print)	Date and Time Notarized _____ ___ _____ am / pm
Phone # / E-mail	Date of document	Witness Phone # / E-mail	Print of Right Thumb
Address	Satisfactory evidence of ID ☐ Driver's license ☐ Known Personally ☐ Credible Witness(es) ☐ Passport ☐ I.D. Card ☐ See Notes	Witness Address	
☐ ID. Issued by ☐ I.D. Number	☐ Expiration Date ☐ Issue Date	Notes	
Signer Signature		Witness Signature	

212

Service: ☐ Acknowledgment ☐ Oath/Affirmation ☐ Jurat ☐ Other/See Notes Fee $_____ Travel_____

Name (print)	Document type /Doc. name	Witness Name (print)	Date and Time Notarized _____ ___ _____ am / pm
Phone # / E-mail	Date of document	Witness Phone # / E-mail	Print of Right Thumb
Address	Satisfactory evidence of ID ☐ Driver's license ☐ Known Personally ☐ Credible Witness(es) ☐ Passport ☐ I.D. Card ☐ See Notes	Witness Address	
☐ ID. Issued by ☐ I.D. Number	☐ Expiration Date ☐ Issue Date	Notes	
Signer Signature		Witness Signature	

NOTARY PUBLIC JOURNAL – LARGE ENTRIES

213
Service: ☐ Acknowledgment ☐ Oath/Affirmation ☐ Jurat ☐ Other/See Notes   Fee $_____   Travel_____

Name (print)	Document type /Doc. name	Witness Name (print)	Date and Time Notarized _____ ___ _____ am / pm
Phone # / E-mail	Date of document	Witness Phone # / E-mail	Print of Right Thumb
Address	Satisfactory evidence of ID ☐ Driver's license ☐ Known Personally ☐ Credible Witness(es) ☐ Passport ☐ I.D. Card ☐ See Notes	Witness Address	
☐ ID. Issued by ☐ I.D. Number	☐ Expiration Date ☐ Issue Date	Notes	
Signer Signature		Witness Signature	

214
Service: ☐ Acknowledgment ☐ Oath/Affirmation ☐ Jurat ☐ Other/See Notes   Fee $_____   Travel_____

Name (print)	Document type /Doc. name	Witness Name (print)	Date and Time Notarized _____ ___ _____ am / pm
Phone # / E-mail	Date of document	Witness Phone # / E-mail	Print of Right Thumb
Address	Satisfactory evidence of ID ☐ Driver's license ☐ Known Personally ☐ Credible Witness(es) ☐ Passport ☐ I.D. Card ☐ See Notes	Witness Address	
☐ ID. Issued by ☐ I.D. Number	☐ Expiration Date ☐ Issue Date	Notes	
Signer Signature		Witness Signature	

NOTARY PUBLIC JOURNAL – LARGE ENTRIES

215

Service: ☐ Acknowledgment ☐ Oath/Affirmation ☐ Jurat ☐ Other/See Notes   Fee $_____   Travel _____

Name (print)	Document type /Doc. name	Witness Name (print)	Date and Time Notarized
			_____ ___ _____ am / pm
Phone # / E-mail	Date of document	Witness Phone # / E-mail	Print of Right Thumb
Address	Satisfactory evidence of ID ☐ Driver's license ☐ Known Personally ☐ Credible Witness(es) ☐ Passport ☐ I.D. Card ☐ See Notes	Witness Address	
☐ ID. Issued by	☐ Expiration Date	Notes	
☐ I.D. Number	☐ Issue Date		
Signer Signature		Witness Signature	

216

Service: ☐ Acknowledgment ☐ Oath/Affirmation ☐ Jurat ☐ Other/See Notes   Fee $_____   Travel _____

Name (print)	Document type /Doc. name	Witness Name (print)	Date and Time Notarized
			_____ ___ _____ am / pm
Phone # / E-mail	Date of document	Witness Phone # / E-mail	Print of Right Thumb
Address	Satisfactory evidence of ID ☐ Driver's license ☐ Known Personally ☐ Credible Witness(es) ☐ Passport ☐ I.D. Card ☐ See Notes	Witness Address	
☐ ID. Issued by	☐ Expiration Date	Notes	
☐ I.D. Number	☐ Issue Date		
Signer Signature		Witness Signature	

NOTARY PUBLIC JOURNAL – LARGE ENTRIES | 111

217
Service: ☐ Acknowledgment ☐ Oath/Affirmation ☐ Jurat ☐ Other/See Notes   Fee $ _____   Travel _____

Name (print)	Document type /Doc. name	Witness Name (print)	Date and Time Notarized
			_____ ___ _____ am / pm
Phone # / E-mail	Date of document	Witness Phone # / E-mail	Print of Right Thumb
Address	Satisfactory evidence of ID ☐ Driver's license ☐ Known Personally ☐ Credible Witness(es) ☐ Passport ☐ I.D. Card ☐ See Notes	Witness Address	
☐ ID. Issued by ☐ I.D. Number	☐ Expiration Date ☐ Issue Date	Notes	
Signer Signature		Witness Signature	

218
Service: ☐ Acknowledgment ☐ Oath/Affirmation ☐ Jurat ☐ Other/See Notes   Fee $ _____   Travel _____

Name (print)	Document type /Doc. name	Witness Name (print)	Date and Time Notarized
			_____ ___ _____ am / pm
Phone # / E-mail	Date of document	Witness Phone # / E-mail	Print of Right Thumb
Address	Satisfactory evidence of ID ☐ Driver's license ☐ Known Personally ☐ Credible Witness(es) ☐ Passport ☐ I.D. Card ☐ See Notes	Witness Address	
☐ ID. Issued by ☐ I.D. Number	☐ Expiration Date ☐ Issue Date	Notes	
Signer Signature		Witness Signature	

NOTARY PUBLIC JOURNAL – LARGE ENTRIES

219
Service: ☐ Acknowledgment ☐ Oath/Affirmation ☐ Jurat ☐ Other/See Notes Fee $_____ Travel_____

Name (print)	Document type /Doc. name	Witness Name (print)	Date and Time Notarized _____ ___ _____ am / pm
Phone # / E-mail	Date of document	Witness Phone # / E-mail	Print of Right Thumb
Address	Satisfactory evidence of ID ☐ Driver's license ☐ Known Personally ☐ Credible Witness(es) ☐ Passport ☐ I.D. Card ☐ See Notes	Witness Address	
☐ ID. Issued by ☐ I.D. Number	☐ Expiration Date ☐ Issue Date	Notes	
Signer Signature		Witness Signature	

220
Service: ☐ Acknowledgment ☐ Oath/Affirmation ☐ Jurat ☐ Other/See Notes Fee $_____ Travel_____

Name (print)	Document type /Doc. name	Witness Name (print)	Date and Time Notarized _____ ___ _____ am / pm
Phone # / E-mail	Date of document	Witness Phone # / E-mail	Print of Right Thumb
Address	Satisfactory evidence of ID ☐ Driver's license ☐ Known Personally ☐ Credible Witness(es) ☐ Passport ☐ I.D. Card ☐ See Notes	Witness Address	
☐ ID. Issued by ☐ I.D. Number	☐ Expiration Date ☐ Issue Date	Notes	
Signer Signature		Witness Signature	

NOTARY PUBLIC JOURNAL – LARGE ENTRIES

221 Service: ☐ Acknowledgment ☐ Oath/Affirmation ☐ Jurat ☐ Other/See Notes Fee $_____ Travel_____

Name (print)	Document type /Doc. name	Witness Name (print)	Date and Time Notarized _____ ___ _____ am / pm
Phone # / E-mail	Date of document	Witness Phone # / E-mail	Print of Right Thumb
Address	Satisfactory evidence of ID ☐ Driver's license ☐ Known Personally ☐ Credible Witness(es) ☐ Passport ☐ I.D. Card ☐ See Notes	Witness Address	
☐ ID. Issued by ☐ I.D. Number	☐ Expiration Date ☐ Issue Date	Notes	
Signer Signature		Witness Signature	

222 Service: ☐ Acknowledgment ☐ Oath/Affirmation ☐ Jurat ☐ Other/See Notes Fee $_____ Travel_____

Name (print)	Document type /Doc. name	Witness Name (print)	Date and Time Notarized _____ ___ _____ am / pm
Phone # / E-mail	Date of document	Witness Phone # / E-mail	Print of Right Thumb
Address	Satisfactory evidence of ID ☐ Driver's license ☐ Known Personally ☐ Credible Witness(es) ☐ Passport ☐ I.D. Card ☐ See Notes	Witness Address	
☐ ID. Issued by ☐ I.D. Number	☐ Expiration Date ☐ Issue Date	Notes	
Signer Signature		Witness Signature	

NOTARY PUBLIC JOURNAL – LARGE ENTRIES

223

Service: ☐ Acknowledgment ☐ Oath/Affirmation ☐ Jurat ☐ Other/See Notes   Fee $_____   Travel_____

Name (print)	Document type /Doc. name	Witness Name (print)	Date and Time Notarized _____ ___ _____ am / pm
Phone # / E-mail	Date of document	Witness Phone # / E-mail	Print of Right Thumb
Address	Satisfactory evidence of ID ☐ Driver's license ☐ Known Personally ☐ Credible Witness(es) ☐ Passport ☐ I.D. Card ☐ See Notes	Witness Address	
☐ ID. Issued by ☐ I.D. Number	☐ Expiration Date ☐ Issue Date	Notes	
Signer Signature		Witness Signature	

224

Service: ☐ Acknowledgment ☐ Oath/Affirmation ☐ Jurat ☐ Other/See Notes   Fee $_____   Travel_____

Name (print)	Document type /Doc. name	Witness Name (print)	Date and Time Notarized _____ ___ _____ am / pm
Phone # / E-mail	Date of document	Witness Phone # / E-mail	Print of Right Thumb
Address	Satisfactory evidence of ID ☐ Driver's license ☐ Known Personally ☐ Credible Witness(es) ☐ Passport ☐ I.D. Card ☐ See Notes	Witness Address	
☐ ID. Issued by ☐ I.D. Number	☐ Expiration Date ☐ Issue Date	Notes	
Signer Signature		Witness Signature	

NOTARY PUBLIC JOURNAL – LARGE ENTRIES | 115

225
Service: ☐ Acknowledgment ☐ Oath/Affirmation ☐ Jurat ☐ Other/See Notes Fee $_____ Travel_____

Name (print)	Document type /Doc. name	Witness Name (print)	Date and Time Notarized _____ ___ _____ am / pm
Phone # / E-mail	Date of document	Witness Phone # / E-mail	Print of Right Thumb
Address	Satisfactory evidence of ID ☐ Driver's license ☐ Known Personally ☐ Credible Witness(es) ☐ Passport ☐ I.D. Card ☐ See Notes	Witness Address	
☐ ID. Issued by ☐ I.D. Number	☐ Expiration Date ☐ Issue Date	Notes	
Signer Signature		Witness Signature	

226
Service: ☐ Acknowledgment ☐ Oath/Affirmation ☐ Jurat ☐ Other/See Notes Fee $_____ Travel_____

Name (print)	Document type /Doc. name	Witness Name (print)	Date and Time Notarized _____ ___ _____ am / pm
Phone # / E-mail	Date of document	Witness Phone # / E-mail	Print of Right Thumb
Address	Satisfactory evidence of ID ☐ Driver's license ☐ Known Personally ☐ Credible Witness(es) ☐ Passport ☐ I.D. Card ☐ See Notes	Witness Address	
☐ ID. Issued by ☐ I.D. Number	☐ Expiration Date ☐ Issue Date	Notes	
Signer Signature		Witness Signature	

116 NOTARY PUBLIC JOURNAL – LARGE ENTRIES

227
Service: ☐ Acknowledgment ☐ Oath/Affirmation ☐ Jurat ☐ Other/See Notes Fee $_____ Travel_____

Name (print)	Document type /Doc. name	Witness Name (print)	Date and Time Notarized _____ ___ _____ am / pm
Phone # / E-mail	Date of document	Witness Phone # / E-mail	Print of Right Thumb
Address	Satisfactory evidence of ID ☐ Driver's license ☐ Known Personally ☐ Credible Witness(es) ☐ Passport ☐ I.D. Card ☐ See Notes	Witness Address	
☐ ID. Issued by ☐ I.D. Number	☐ Expiration Date ☐ Issue Date	Notes	
Signer Signature		Witness Signature	

228
Service: ☐ Acknowledgment ☐ Oath/Affirmation ☐ Jurat ☐ Other/See Notes Fee $_____ Travel_____

Name (print)	Document type /Doc. name	Witness Name (print)	Date and Time Notarized _____ ___ _____ am / pm
Phone # / E-mail	Date of document	Witness Phone # / E-mail	Print of Right Thumb
Address	Satisfactory evidence of ID ☐ Driver's license ☐ Known Personally ☐ Credible Witness(es) ☐ Passport ☐ I.D. Card ☐ See Notes	Witness Address	
☐ ID. Issued by ☐ I.D. Number	☐ Expiration Date ☐ Issue Date	Notes	
Signer Signature		Witness Signature	

NOTARY PUBLIC JOURNAL – LARGE ENTRIES | 117

229

Service: ☐ Acknowledgment ☐ Oath/Affirmation ☐ Jurat ☐ Other/See Notes Fee $_____ Travel_____

Name (print)	Document type /Doc. name	Witness Name (print)	Date and Time Notarized _____ ___ _____ am / pm
Phone # / E-mail	Date of document	Witness Phone # / E-mail	Print of Right Thumb
Address	Satisfactory evidence of ID ☐ Driver's license ☐ Known Personally ☐ Credible Witness(es) ☐ Passport ☐ I.D. Card ☐ See Notes	Witness Address	
☐ ID. Issued by ☐ I.D. Number	☐ Expiration Date ☐ Issue Date	Notes	
Signer Signature		Witness Signature	

230

Service: ☐ Acknowledgment ☐ Oath/Affirmation ☐ Jurat ☐ Other/See Notes Fee $_____ Travel_____

Name (print)	Document type /Doc. name	Witness Name (print)	Date and Time Notarized _____ ___ _____ am / pm
Phone # / E-mail	Date of document	Witness Phone # / E-mail	Print of Right Thumb
Address	Satisfactory evidence of ID ☐ Driver's license ☐ Known Personally ☐ Credible Witness(es) ☐ Passport ☐ I.D. Card ☐ See Notes	Witness Address	
☐ ID. Issued by ☐ I.D. Number	☐ Expiration Date ☐ Issue Date	Notes	
Signer Signature		Witness Signature	

NOTARY PUBLIC JOURNAL – LARGE ENTRIES

231
Service: ☐ Acknowledgment ☐ Oath/Affirmation ☐ Jurat ☐ Other/See Notes Fee $_____ Travel_____

Name (print)	Document type /Doc. name	Witness Name (print)	Date and Time Notarized _____ ___ _____ am / pm
Phone # / E-mail	Date of document	Witness Phone # / E-mail	Print of Right Thumb
Address	Satisfactory evidence of ID ☐ Driver's license ☐ Known Personally ☐ Credible Witness(es) ☐ Passport ☐ I.D. Card ☐ See Notes	Witness Address	
☐ ID. Issued by ☐ I.D. Number	☐ Expiration Date ☐ Issue Date	Notes	
Signer Signature		Witness Signature	

232
Service: ☐ Acknowledgment ☐ Oath/Affirmation ☐ Jurat ☐ Other/See Notes Fee $_____ Travel_____

Name (print)	Document type /Doc. name	Witness Name (print)	Date and Time Notarized _____ ___ _____ am / pm
Phone # / E-mail	Date of document	Witness Phone # / E-mail	Print of Right Thumb
Address	Satisfactory evidence of ID ☐ Driver's license ☐ Known Personally ☐ Credible Witness(es) ☐ Passport ☐ I.D. Card ☐ See Notes	Witness Address	
☐ ID. Issued by ☐ I.D. Number	☐ Expiration Date ☐ Issue Date	Notes	
Signer Signature		Witness Signature	

NOTARY PUBLIC JOURNAL – LARGE ENTRIES | 119

233
Service: ☐ Acknowledgment ☐ Oath/Affirmation ☐ Jurat ☐ Other/See Notes   Fee $_____ Travel_____

Name (print)	Document type /Doc. name	Witness Name (print)	Date and Time Notarized _____ ___ _____ am / pm
Phone # / E-mail	Date of document	Witness Phone # / E-mail	Print of Right Thumb
Address	Satisfactory evidence of ID ☐ Driver's license ☐ Known Personally ☐ Credible Witness(es) ☐ Passport ☐ I.D. Card ☐ See Notes	Witness Address	
☐ ID. Issued by ☐ I.D. Number	☐ Expiration Date ☐ Issue Date	Notes	
Signer Signature		Witness Signature	

234
Service: ☐ Acknowledgment ☐ Oath/Affirmation ☐ Jurat ☐ Other/See Notes   Fee $_____ Travel_____

Name (print)	Document type /Doc. name	Witness Name (print)	Date and Time Notarized _____ ___ _____ am / pm
Phone # / E-mail	Date of document	Witness Phone # / E-mail	Print of Right Thumb
Address	Satisfactory evidence of ID ☐ Driver's license ☐ Known Personally ☐ Credible Witness(es) ☐ Passport ☐ I.D. Card ☐ See Notes	Witness Address	
☐ ID. Issued by ☐ I.D. Number	☐ Expiration Date ☐ Issue Date	Notes	
Signer Signature		Witness Signature	

NOTARY PUBLIC JOURNAL – LARGE ENTRIES

235
Service: ☐ Acknowledgment ☐ Oath/Affirmation ☐ Jurat ☐ Other/See Notes   Fee $ _____   Travel _____

Name (print)	Document type /Doc. name	Witness Name (print)	Date and Time Notarized
			_____ ___ _____ am / pm
Phone # / E-mail	Date of document	Witness Phone # / E-mail	Print of Right Thumb
Address	Satisfactory evidence of ID ☐ Driver's license ☐ Known Personally ☐ Credible Witness(es) ☐ Passport ☐ I.D. Card ☐ See Notes	Witness Address	
☐ ID. Issued by ☐ I.D. Number	☐ Expiration Date ☐ Issue Date	Notes	
Signer Signature		Witness Signature	

236
Service: ☐ Acknowledgment ☐ Oath/Affirmation ☐ Jurat ☐ Other/See Notes   Fee $ _____   Travel _____

Name (print)	Document type /Doc. name	Witness Name (print)	Date and Time Notarized
			_____ ___ _____ am / pm
Phone # / E-mail	Date of document	Witness Phone # / E-mail	Print of Right Thumb
Address	Satisfactory evidence of ID ☐ Driver's license ☐ Known Personally ☐ Credible Witness(es) ☐ Passport ☐ I.D. Card ☐ See Notes	Witness Address	
☐ ID. Issued by ☐ I.D. Number	☐ Expiration Date ☐ Issue Date	Notes	
Signer Signature		Witness Signature	

NOTARY PUBLIC JOURNAL – LARGE ENTRIES | 121

237

Service: ☐ Acknowledgment ☐ Oath/Affirmation ☐ Jurat ☐ Other/See Notes   Fee $_____   Travel_____

Name (print)	Document type /Doc. name	Witness Name (print)	Date and Time Notarized _____ ___ _____ am / pm
Phone # / E-mail	Date of document	Witness Phone # / E-mail	Print of Right Thumb
Address	Satisfactory evidence of ID ☐ Driver's license ☐ Known Personally ☐ Credible Witness(es) ☐ Passport ☐ I.D. Card ☐ See Notes	Witness Address	
☐ ID. Issued by ☐ I.D. Number	☐ Expiration Date ☐ Issue Date	Notes	
Signer Signature		Witness Signature	

238

Service: ☐ Acknowledgment ☐ Oath/Affirmation ☐ Jurat ☐ Other/See Notes   Fee $_____   Travel_____

Name (print)	Document type /Doc. name	Witness Name (print)	Date and Time Notarized _____ ___ _____ am / pm
Phone # / E-mail	Date of document	Witness Phone # / E-mail	Print of Right Thumb
Address	Satisfactory evidence of ID ☐ Driver's license ☐ Known Personally ☐ Credible Witness(es) ☐ Passport ☐ I.D. Card ☐ See Notes	Witness Address	
☐ ID. Issued by ☐ I.D. Number	☐ Expiration Date ☐ Issue Date	Notes	
Signer Signature		Witness Signature	

NOTARY PUBLIC JOURNAL – LARGE ENTRIES

239
Service: ☐ Acknowledgment ☐ Oath/Affirmation ☐ Jurat ☐ Other/See Notes   Fee $_____   Travel_____

Name (print)	Document type /Doc. name	Witness Name (print)	Date and Time Notarized _____ ___ _____ am / pm
Phone # / E-mail	Date of document	Witness Phone # / E-mail	Print of Right Thumb
Address	Satisfactory evidence of ID ☐ Driver's license ☐ Known Personally ☐ Credible Witness(es) ☐ Passport ☐ I.D. Card ☐ See Notes	Witness Address	
☐ ID. Issued by ☐ I.D. Number	☐ Expiration Date ☐ Issue Date	Notes	
Signer Signature		Witness Signature	

240
Service: ☐ Acknowledgment ☐ Oath/Affirmation ☐ Jurat ☐ Other/See Notes   Fee $_____   Travel_____

Name (print)	Document type /Doc. name	Witness Name (print)	Date and Time Notarized _____ ___ _____ am / pm
Phone # / E-mail	Date of document	Witness Phone # / E-mail	Print of Right Thumb
Address	Satisfactory evidence of ID ☐ Driver's license ☐ Known Personally ☐ Credible Witness(es) ☐ Passport ☐ I.D. Card ☐ See Notes	Witness Address	
☐ ID. Issued by ☐ I.D. Number	☐ Expiration Date ☐ Issue Date	Notes	
Signer Signature		Witness Signature	

NOTARY PUBLIC JOURNAL – LARGE ENTRIES | 123

241
Service: ☐ Acknowledgment ☐ Oath/Affirmation ☐ Jurat ☐ Other/See Notes   Fee $_____ Travel_____

Name (print)	Document type /Doc. name	Witness Name (print)	Date and Time Notarized _____ ___ _____ am / pm
Phone # / E-mail	Date of document	Witness Phone # / E-mail	Print of Right Thumb
Address	Satisfactory evidence of ID ☐ Driver's license ☐ Known Personally ☐ Credible Witness(es) ☐ Passport ☐ I.D. Card ☐ See Notes	Witness Address	
☐ ID. Issued by ☐ I.D. Number	☐ Expiration Date ☐ Issue Date	Notes	
Signer Signature		Witness Signature	

242
Service: ☐ Acknowledgment ☐ Oath/Affirmation ☐ Jurat ☐ Other/See Notes   Fee $_____ Travel_____

Name (print)	Document type /Doc. name	Witness Name (print)	Date and Time Notarized _____ ___ _____ am / pm
Phone # / E-mail	Date of document	Witness Phone # / E-mail	Print of Right Thumb
Address	Satisfactory evidence of ID ☐ Driver's license ☐ Known Personally ☐ Credible Witness(es) ☐ Passport ☐ I.D. Card ☐ See Notes	Witness Address	
☐ ID. Issued by ☐ I.D. Number	☐ Expiration Date ☐ Issue Date	Notes	
Signer Signature		Witness Signature	

NOTARY PUBLIC JOURNAL – LARGE ENTRIES

243 Service: ☐ Acknowledgment ☐ Oath/Affirmation ☐ Jurat ☐ Other/See Notes   Fee $_____   Travel_____

Name (print)	Document type /Doc. name	Witness Name (print)	Date and Time Notarized _____ ___ _____ am / pm
Phone # / E-mail	Date of document	Witness Phone # / E-mail	Print of Right Thumb
Address	Satisfactory evidence of ID ☐ Driver's license ☐ Known Personally ☐ Credible Witness(es) ☐ Passport ☐ I.D. Card ☐ See Notes	Witness Address	
☐ ID. Issued by ☐ I.D. Number	☐ Expiration Date ☐ Issue Date	Notes	
Signer Signature		Witness Signature	

244 Service: ☐ Acknowledgment ☐ Oath/Affirmation ☐ Jurat ☐ Other/See Notes   Fee $_____   Travel_____

Name (print)	Document type /Doc. name	Witness Name (print)	Date and Time Notarized _____ ___ _____ am / pm
Phone # / E-mail	Date of document	Witness Phone # / E-mail	Print of Right Thumb
Address	Satisfactory evidence of ID ☐ Driver's license ☐ Known Personally ☐ Credible Witness(es) ☐ Passport ☐ I.D. Card ☐ See Notes	Witness Address	
☐ ID. Issued by ☐ I.D. Number	☐ Expiration Date ☐ Issue Date	Notes	
Signer Signature		Witness Signature	

NOTARY PUBLIC JOURNAL – LARGE ENTRIES | 125

245
Service: ☐ Acknowledgment ☐ Oath/Affirmation ☐ Jurat ☐ Other/See Notes   Fee $_____   Travel_____

Name (print)	Document type /Doc. name	Witness Name (print)	Date and Time Notarized _____ ___ _____ am / pm
Phone # / E-mail	Date of document	Witness Phone # / E-mail	Print of Right Thumb
Address	Satisfactory evidence of ID ☐ Driver's license ☐ Known Personally ☐ Credible Witness(es) ☐ Passport ☐ I.D. Card ☐ See Notes	Witness Address	
☐ ID. Issued by ☐ I.D. Number	☐ Expiration Date ☐ Issue Date	Notes	
Signer Signature		Witness Signature	

246
Service: ☐ Acknowledgment ☐ Oath/Affirmation ☐ Jurat ☐ Other/See Notes   Fee $_____   Travel_____

Name (print)	Document type /Doc. name	Witness Name (print)	Date and Time Notarized _____ ___ _____ am / pm
Phone # / E-mail	Date of document	Witness Phone # / E-mail	Print of Right Thumb
Address	Satisfactory evidence of ID ☐ Driver's license ☐ Known Personally ☐ Credible Witness(es) ☐ Passport ☐ I.D. Card ☐ See Notes	Witness Address	
☐ ID. Issued by ☐ I.D. Number	☐ Expiration Date ☐ Issue Date	Notes	
Signer Signature		Witness Signature	

NOTARY PUBLIC JOURNAL – LARGE ENTRIES

247

Service: ☐ Acknowledgment ☐ Oath/Affirmation ☐ Jurat ☐ Other/See Notes   Fee $_____   Travel_____

Name (print)	Document type /Doc. name	Witness Name (print)	Date and Time Notarized _____ ___ _____ am / pm
Phone # / E-mail	Date of document	Witness Phone # / E-mail	Print of Right Thumb
Address	Satisfactory evidence of ID ☐ Driver's license ☐ Known Personally ☐ Credible Witness(es) ☐ Passport ☐ I.D. Card ☐ See Notes	Witness Address	
☐ ID. Issued by ☐ I.D. Number	☐ Expiration Date ☐ Issue Date	Notes	
Signer Signature		Witness Signature	

248

Service: ☐ Acknowledgment ☐ Oath/Affirmation ☐ Jurat ☐ Other/See Notes   Fee $_____   Travel_____

Name (print)	Document type /Doc. name	Witness Name (print)	Date and Time Notarized _____ ___ _____ am / pm
Phone # / E-mail	Date of document	Witness Phone # / E-mail	Print of Right Thumb
Address	Satisfactory evidence of ID ☐ Driver's license ☐ Known Personally ☐ Credible Witness(es) ☐ Passport ☐ I.D. Card ☐ See Notes	Witness Address	
☐ ID. Issued by ☐ I.D. Number	☐ Expiration Date ☐ Issue Date	Notes	
Signer Signature		Witness Signature	

NOTARY PUBLIC JOURNAL – LARGE ENTRIES

249
Service: ☐ Acknowledgment ☐ Oath/Affirmation ☐ Jurat ☐ Other/See Notes Fee $_____ Travel_____

Name (print)	Document type /Doc. name	Witness Name (print)	Date and Time Notarized _____ ___ _____ am / pm
Phone # / E-mail	Date of document	Witness Phone # / E-mail	Print of Right Thumb
Address	Satisfactory evidence of ID ☐ Driver's license ☐ Known Personally ☐ Credible Witness(es) ☐ Passport ☐ I.D. Card ☐ See Notes	Witness Address	
☐ ID. Issued by ☐ I.D. Number	☐ Expiration Date ☐ Issue Date	Notes	
Signer Signature		Witness Signature	

250
Service: ☐ Acknowledgment ☐ Oath/Affirmation ☐ Jurat ☐ Other/See Notes Fee $_____ Travel_____

Name (print)	Document type /Doc. name	Witness Name (print)	Date and Time Notarized _____ ___ _____ am / pm
Phone # / E-mail	Date of document	Witness Phone # / E-mail	Print of Right Thumb
Address	Satisfactory evidence of ID ☐ Driver's license ☐ Known Personally ☐ Credible Witness(es) ☐ Passport ☐ I.D. Card ☐ See Notes	Witness Address	
☐ ID. Issued by ☐ I.D. Number	☐ Expiration Date ☐ Issue Date	Notes	
Signer Signature		Witness Signature	

* Quote on pg. 2 is from Wikipedia.org

Made in the
USA
Monee, IL

15696214R00072